Triathlon
Technique
Training
Competition

Martin Engelhardt and Alexandra Kremer

translated by Andrew Shackleton

 Springfield Books Limited

Published by Springfield Books Limited,
Norman Road, Denby Dale,
Huddersfield HD8 8TH, West Yorkshire,
Great Britain

Original text copyright © 1987
BLV Verlagsgesellschaft mbH, München,
8000 München 40, West Germany

English translation copyright © 1989
Springfield Books Limited,
Norman Road, Denby Dale,
Huddersfield HD8 8TH, West Yorkshire,
Great Britain

First edition 1989

British Library Cataloguing in Publication
Data
Engelhardt, Martin
Triathlon: technique, training and
competition.
1. Triathlon
I. Title II. Kremer, Alexandra III.
[Triathlon perfekt].
English
796

ISBN: 0 947655 53 0

Acknowledgements

Illustrations: Barbara von Damnitz
Cover design: Douglas Martin Associates
Translation: Andrew Shackleton
Technical advisers on English edition:
  Andrew Widgery, Dick Poole and
  Pauline Carter
Typesetting: Armitage Typo/Graphics
Printed in England by The Bath Press

Photographic Credits

Graham Watson: cover photographs, and
  the pictures on pages 13 (left) and 15
Archiv Arena: page 18 (top)
Archiv Le Coq Sportif: frontispiece,
  pages 36, 78, 146
Archiv Look: page 20
D. Birkner: pages 17, 18 (bottom), 19, 23,
  25, 28, 32, 33, 50, 80/81, 82/83, 84/85, 87,
  89, 90
H. J. Herzog: page 12
Kent: page 54
G. Klaeren: page 108
T. Kleine-Rüschkamp: pages 16, 105
Th. Knoeckel: page 51
Ch. Khün: pages 65, 128/129
Pühn/Lutz (*Hilpoltsteiner Volkszeitung*):
  pages 13 (right), 14, 63, 67, 95, 96/97,
  104, 105 (top), 106, 133
M. Sauerbier: page 135
E. D. Schmickler: pages 11, 103
Schlüssler: page 25
K. Steinbach: page 42
H. Szware: pages 8, 79, 98

Source Credits

(*Italic* numbers = graphs and diagrams;
bold numbers = tables; ordinary
numbers = textual material)

D. Bremer *Triathlon Training* (Hessischer
  Triathlon Verband, Darmstadt 1985):
  pages 59-61
M. Grosser/A. Neumaier *Techniktraining*
  (BLV Verlagsgesellschaft, Munich 1982):
  page *67*
M. Grosser et al *Konditionstraining* (BLV
  Verlagsgesellschaft, Munich 1985):
  pages 55, **57, 59,** 79, 81
D. Harre *Trainingslehre* (Sportverlag, Berlin
  1977): pages *57,* **94, 97**
S. Israel in *Medizin und Sport* 16:1 (1976):
  page **96**
R. Kilzer/B. Zollfrank *Radsport* (Limpert
  Verlag, Frankfurt/Main 1984): page *66*
P. Konopka *Sporternährung* (BLV
  Verlagsgesellschaft, Munich 1985):
  pages 96–97, **110, 111,** *112,* **112,** 116
H. de Marées *Sportphysiologie*
  (Troponwerke, Cologne 1976):
  pages *77, 119*
K. H. Ricken/W. Kindermann in *Sonderheft
  Deutsche Zeitschrift für Sportmedizin* 37
  (1986): page 127
D. Samulski in *Sportpsychologie* 1:1 (1987):
  page 101
J. Weinek *Optimales Training* (Perimed,
  Erlangen 1983): page 79
E./T. Wessinghage *Laufen* (BLV
  Verlagsgesellschaft, Munich 1987):
  pages **113, 114, 115**

Contents

Introduction   9

Why the triathlon?   9
The development of the triathlon   10
A historical survey   12
Triathlon series   15
People's triathlon   15
Youth events   15
Multiple endurance competitions   16

Equipment   17

Swimming   17
Cycling   18
The frame   19
The steering   21
The transmission   22
The wheels   25
The tyres   26
The brakes   28
The saddle   28
Accessories   29
The right saddle position   29
Bicycle maintenance   31
Indoor training aids   32
Clothing for training   33
Running   34
Running shoes   34
Clothing for training   35

Technique   37

Technical training   37
Swimming   39
The physics of swimming   39
The crawl stroke   40
Learning exercises   42
Cycling   45
The physics of cycling   45
Riding posture   46
Round pedalling   46
The best pedalling rate   47
Climbing position   49
Cornering   49
Dealing with obstacles   50
Running   51
Technical description   51
Improvement exercises   52

Training   55

Overcompensation   55
Aspects of physical load   56
Principles of progressive overload .   57
Long-term training   58
Basic/Build-up training   58
Competitive and high-performance training   58
Planning and periodisation   61
Preparation period   61
Competition period   62
Transition period   62

A top triathlete's training year   64
The training year for a competitive amateur   64
Training for the non-competitive triathlete   66
Detailed training structure   66
Individual high-performance training   67
Training examples   68
Endurance training   75
Physiological adaptation   75
Training methods   76
Strength training   78
Training methods   78
Circuit training   80
Muscular endurance exercises   82
Flexibility training   87
Loosening-up exercises   88
Stretching exercises   89
Keeping records   90
Overtraining   94

Competition   99

Physical preparation   99
Mental preparation   100
Motivation   100
Coping with pressure   101
The competition day   102
Competition checklist   102
The sequence of events   103

The recovery period 106
Diet 106
Fluid intake 106
Active and passive regeneration.... 107
Progressive muscular relaxation ... 107

Medical aspects   109

Diet and nutrition 109
Carbohydrates 109
Fats 109
Proteins 110
Water 111

Vitamins.................................... 112
Minerals and trace elements......... 113
General nutritional advice 114
Pre-competition diet.................... 114
Diet on the day........................... 116
Hot weather.......................... 116
Rules for competing in hot weather 117
Swimming in cold water 118
Jet lag 118
Drugs and medicines............. 118
Digestive problems................ 122
Injuries.................................. 123
Overuse injuries 123

Acute injuries 125
Colds and other infections 127
Women's problems 127
Medical examination 129

Appendix   131

Organising a triathlon event... 131
A triathlon management plan 136
Triathlon rules 138
Index 141

Foreword

The triathlon is very much the sport of the future, and has made tremendous strides since its inception in the late seventies. Indeed, it is likely to be a ''demonstration'' sport in the 1992 Olympic Games, and possibly a full Olympic sport in 1996 – a record in itself.

This intriguing event combines all the elements that go to make up a true all rounder – speed, strength, skill, stamina and not a little determination. Today's top triathletes have attained the very highest levels of athleticism by sheer hard work and application, coupled with unbelievable enthusiasm.

However, the triathlon isn't just for super-stars; it presents a very real but attainable challenge to the average person who likes to keep fit. For most, just to complete a triathlon is sufficiently satisfying – at first! But such is the nature of the sport that, once you have met that first challenge, you know you can do better and really get ''hooked''.

I well remember seeing my first triathlon and, as a competitive cyclist and coach, watching the efforts of runners and swimmers as they mounted their bicycles. It was obvious that most of them were completely ignorant regarding the cycling phase of the event, and were severely handicapped just by the lack of quite basic knowledge. Today's triathletes are very discerning in their choice of equipment, and top triathletes give the best cyclists a good run for their money. On the other side of the coin, I have painful memories of my first year of training for running, marred once again by a lack of basic information.

In those days there was little or no material available on the triathlon. Most competitors worked on the principle of doing as much training as was humanly possible in each disclipine – in other words, combining the training programmes of top performers in each of the sports, and usually with disastrous results.

Even a cursory glance through the pages of this book reveals that there is a wealth of knowledge here for novice, ''fun-runner'' and aspiring champion alike. It's a must for anyone interested in the sport, and a valuable source of information to which to refer when compiling training programmes or correcting faults.

Dick Poole

Chairman,
British Triathlon Association, 1983–1989
National Coach,
Road Time Trials Council, 1966–1978
Honorary Treasurer,
European Triathlon Union, 1984–1989

Introcuction

Why the triathlon?

The triathlon can be defined quite simply. It is a continuous endurance event made up of the three elements of swimming, cycling and running. It is continuous in that the stopwatch never stops, from the start of the swimming right up until the last competitor has run past the finishing post.

The triathlon has become so enormously popular over recent years that there must be some reason for this boom. What, then, is the secret of the triathlon? Is it just a passing whim of fashion? Or is it rather because it fulfils the particular leisure requirements of the health-conscious eighties?

Last year more than a million people took part in triathlon events worldwide. There is a wide choice of competitive levels available. At the bottom end of the scale is the "One-tenth Ironman" on the island of Lanzarote, which has provided nearly a thousand energetic holidaymakers with their first taste of the triathlon. Working up the scale, there are the people's triathlon, the short, middle and long events, and finally the top-distance races in Hawaii, Holland, England and elsewhere. There is something for every ability level in a sport that is open to young and old, male and female alike. Where else is there a sport that can accommodate so many levels at the same time?

Such a varied programme relies for its success upon the backing of a well-regulated organisational structure. This too has been achieved. The British umbrella organisation is the British Triathlon Association (BTA). Apart from organising the British Championships, the BTA lays down a code of rules, which is chiefly designed to ensure safety, fair play and equality of opportunity. The triathlon is organised locally by a number of regional bodies. These are responsible for supervising the activities of the local clubs, organising regional championships and coordinating the timetable of events.

Lack of resources in the past has inevitably limited some of the essential spadework such as spotting and encouraging talent among young competitors. But British and European Championships have been held annually since 1985. The proportion of women competitors is only ten per cent in Great Britain as opposed to thirty per cent in the United States.

Lack of physical activity is one of the main causes of heart and circulatory diseases – a major cause of death in the Western world. Endurance training may not be a recipe for immortality, but it is without doubt the best way of prolonging your life to its full potential span. This depends, however, on a regular training programme. Endurance training should be planned as part of your everyday schedule of activities, like eating, drinking or brushing your teeth.

The activities of swimming, cycling and running can be varied – depending on individual choice and the time of year – to include a whole range of other sports such as cross-country skiing, rollerskating, ice-skating or canoeing. This will not only ensure a basic level of endurance for all sporting activities, but will bring about a general improvement in health and quality of life. Triathlon training is full of variety, and the excitement of competitions provides further motivation.

What, then, is the distinction between all-round and high-performance sports training? Basically, high-performance training goes beyond the minimum level of training that is considered essential to health from a medical point of view. This minimum usually lies somewhere between three and four hours a week.

The modern working day is more conducive to mental rather than physical exhaustion. Swimming, cycling and running provide just the antidote that is needed to such a situation. After only a short time you no longer feel so tired, and your mind is set free for creative mental activity. You can work off your aggressions, achieve greater peace of mind and improve your ability to deal with stress. Endurance activities encourage meditation, positive introspection and inner serenity. For young people who are not yet faced with physical limitations, these positive mental influences are possibly one of the most important health benefits of the triathlon.

The triathlon is not only fun, it is a wonderful adventure! The BTA's executive committee know this from personal experience, as all of them are practising triathletes. Many British athletes have taken part in the famous Ironman in Hawaii. They have swum in the warm crystal-clear waters of the bay of Kona, among the beautiful fishes and corals. They have ridden against the wind for 180 km across the scorched lava wastes of the interior before tackling the final marathon. The faster competitors finish in the daylight, while for most the race goes on into the twilight, with the phosphorescent light playing around their wrists. But everyone feels that glowing sense of achievement at the end. Most can look forward to an exciting adventure. Only the first 100 or 200 triathletes need worry about the final result, because for them every minute is crucial.

The triathlon is a unique combination of experiences. It involves group activity in the open air and pushing your body to its very limits. Even children participating for the first time can enjoy the same sense of achievement as in the Ironman. "It feels as though you've done something really worth doing!" they will say after finishing 200 m of swimming, 8 km of cycling and 2 km of running. They have pushed themselves to their own limits, and are proud of what they have achieved. When you are "burnt out" after a long triathlon, you only have two ideas in your head: a shower and a drink of water. But when you are finally standing under the shower, you are suddenly thrilled with the sense of what you have achieved.

The triathlon is an individual sport, but involves a group awareness that is matched in few other sports. The experience of training and competing together provides a wonderful sense of give and take and mutual concern. The triathlon is a social event too.

There is the delightful experience of swimming in many different environments, from the crystal-clear quarry lakes of Leicester to the Atlantic breakers off Hilton Head, with water temperatures varying between 13° and 26°C. Cycling routes are sometimes flat like Milton Keynes, Peterborough or Southport, sometimes hilly like Winchester or Otley in the Yorkshire Dales, and sometimes through cities such as London or Canterbury. Each scene is a new experience in itself that enriches the excitement of the race.

Running and cycling give an entirely different perspective on nature. While cycling provides a medley of different impressions, running allows one to appreciate the environment in greater detail – the animals and plants in the woods, the scents of flowers and fruits, the sea air with its subtle blend of seaweed and fish. There is heat, cold, rain, snow, asphalt, sand and springy woodland turf – the list is endless. One could scarcely imagine a more intense experience of nature.

The triathlon has so much to offer from the point of view of both health and enjoyment that it will soon achieve full recognition at all levels within the varied programme of sporting events. So fascinating is this sport that one hardly need ask the question "Why the triathlon?"

The development of the triathlon

People have become increasingly health-conscious over recent years, and this has resulted in a greater interest in active participation in sports. This is especially true of endurance sports such as swimming, cycling, running and cyclo-cross.

The origins of the triathlon possibly go back to 1968, with the appearance in America of Kenneth Cooper's book *Aerobics.* The health programme that Dr Cooper proposed was specifically centred around regular endurance training. Of particular interest was a long list of different sports to which points were allocated on the basis of the extent to which they could improve a person's endurance capabilities. At the top of the list were the three sports of swimming, cycling and running.

All three sports had a well-established programme of events at all competitive levels. *Swimming,* for example, is not only the sport of holidaymakers wishing to combine sea, sun and fresh air. It has for several years been one of our country's most popular sporting activities.

Since the late sixties, *running* has seen a massive surge in popularity throughout the industrialised world. Jogging, as it is known, provides a much-needed antidote to the physical inactivity of modern life. In Great Britain alone there are many hundreds of thousands of people who go jogging at least twice a week. Running is possible at all times, in all places and in all weathers. No specialised knowledge or skills are required, and no equipment is needed apart from clothing. Since 1963 there have been regular organised marathons in which everyone can take part.

Cycling has also become very much more popular since the seventies. The two areas of greatest interest have been cycle touring and cycle racing, each of them on machines specially made for the purpose. Weekend touring events are organised during summer months, providing the cyclist's equivalent of the marathon.

At the beginning of the eighties these three sports were combined to create an entirely new endurance event called the triathlon. The triathlon broke completely new ground in the area of endurance.

By combining the three disciplines of swimming, cycling and running, athletes were able to push their endurance capabilities way beyond anything that had previously been achieved.

According to the rules of the British Triathlon Association (BTA), the triathlon sport is graded according to the course distances at the various events. There are the people's triathlon and the short, middle and long triathlon. The course distances of the component disciplines should be in the approximate ratio 1:30–50:9–11. This is to ensure that

specialists in the three disciplines are not specially favoured or disadvantaged. Since 1985 the BTA has ensured that a single code of rules is applied.

The best-known and most spectacular of all triathlon events is the Ironman on Hawaii, which has been held annually since 1978. With course distances of 3.8 km (swimming), 180 km (cycling) and 42.195 km (running), it vies with the rival event at Nice in France (3 km swimming, 120 km cycling, 32 km running) as the unofficial world championship.

The start of the Ironman – Hawaii's classic triathlon event.

At first the newspapers made a lot of the daring nature of the enterprise, with headlines such as "Great Superman Show", "Totally Mad", "Completely Insane" or "Not for Normal People". But such comments are now a thing of the past, for since then the triathlon has become a worldwide phenomenon. Nowadays we see more and more athletes from other sports being encouraged to take part in the triathlon. It is the fastest-growing sport in Great Britain, with a hundredfold increase in the number of participants in the five years from 1983 to 1988.

The development of the triathlon in Great Britain

Year	Number of events	Number of participants
1983	12	250
1984	25	400
1985	40	1,200
1986	70	3,500
1987	90	10,000
1988	140	12,000

A historical survey

Before 1974 Survival trials were instituted in North America, including the *Alaska Trial* and the *Arizona Trial.* The aim of a trial was to cross a state by various means – whether on foot, by canoe, by dogsleigh, on skis or whatever – but without any help from other people. This multi-discipline concept was taken over by the growing number of fitness enthusiasts, joggers and cyclists, and this led eventually to the creation of a new sport called the triathlon.

1974 The first triathlon at San Diego, California. The course distances were 1.5 km swimming, 40 km cycling and 10 km running. The winner was Bill Philipps.

1977 One evening, so we are told, John Collins was having a few pints with some of his friends in a US Army Unit stationed in Hawaii. They were arguing about which was the most gruelling of the three annual endurance events held on the island of Oahu: the Waikiki Roughwater Swim (2.4 mi/3.8 km), the Around Oahu Bike Race (112 mi/180 km) or the Honolulu Marathon. This led to the idea of a single endurance event in which all three competitions were run consecutively on a single day.

1978 On 18 February, fifteen men began the first *Hawaii Triathlon,* or *Ironman.* Twelve of them reached the finish, and the winner was Gordon Haller with a time of 11:46:58.

Dave Scott – five times winner of the Ironman.

1980 On 10 January, the third *Ironman* was broadcast by ABC, the American TV network. Thus the Ironman gained worldwide popularity. The men's champion was Dave Scott with a time of 9:24:33, while the women's champion was Robin Beck with 11:21:24.
21 June was the occasion of the first triathlon in Europe, which was held in the Soviet Union.

1981 On 5 September, the first European triathlon over Ironman-type distances was held at The Hague. The winner was Gregor Stam of the Netherlands with a time of 11:11.

1982 The *Ironman* entered the international headlines when Julie Moss collapsed in front of the TV cameras only minutes from winning the event. She was forced to crawl to the finish, while her rival Kathleen McCartney overtook her only metres from the touchline and won the fifth Ironman with a time of 11:09:40.
America held its first *United States Triathlon Series (USTS).* This consisted of five events based at San Diego, San Francisco, Los Angeles, Seattle and Portland respectively. The distances were 2 km swimming, 40 km cycling and 15 km running.
In December of this year about forty people attended the inaugural meeting of the *British Triathlon Association (BTA).*

1983 By the end of 1983, the membership of the BTA had risen to 200, and about a dozen events had been promoted during the year, including the first *British Short Course National Championship.*

1984 The *European Triathlon Union (ETU)* was formed. Three European Championship events were to be held annually, over short, middle and long distances respectively. An additional team event called the triathlon relay was to be organised during the pre-season period.

The first *London – Paris* team-relay event was held, and BTA membership had doubled to 400. Great Britain was a founder member of the ETU, and the BTA Chairman, Dick Poole, was elected as ETU Treasurer.

1985 The first official *European Championships* (short triathlon) were held at Immenstadt. The distances were 1.3 km swimming, 60 km cycling and 12.3 km running. The men's champion was Rob Barel (NL) with 2:37:42. Alexandra Kremer (WG) won the women's event with 3:06:02.

Great Britain sent teams to this event and to the team relay in Northern Ireland. Sarah Coope, a junior in her first season, came third at Immenstadt.

1986 In May, Great Britain hosted the European Short Course Championship, and later that year the last of the European Team Relay Championships, which were discontinued.

Left: Britain's Sarah Coope, triple European Champion in 1987.

Right: Scott Tinley is one of America's greatest athletes. Among his several achievements are two Ironman victories.

Winners of the Ironman on Hawaii

Men

Year	Name	Swimming	Cycling	Running	Totals
1978	Gordon Haller	–	–	–	11:46:58
1979	Tom Warren	1:06:15	6:19	3:51	11:15:56
1980	Dave Scott	0:51	5:03	3:30:33	9:24:33
1981	John Howard	1:11:12	5:03:29	3:23:48	9:38:29
1982 (Feb)	Scott Tinley	1:10:45	5:05:11	3:03:45	9:19:41
1982 (Oct)	Dave Scott	0:50:52	5:10:16	3:07:15	9:08:23
1983	Dave Scott	0:50:52	5:10:48	3:04:16	9:05:57
1984	Dave Scott	0:50:21.4	5:10:59.1	2:53:00.2	8:54:20.7
1985	Scott Tinley	0:55:13	4:54:07	3:01:33	8:50:54
1986	Dave Scott	0:50:53.8	4:48:32.2	2:49:11.5	8:28:37.5
1987	Dave Scott	0:57:00	4:53:48	2:49:26	8:34:13
1988	Scott Molina	0:51:28:00	4:36:50	3:02:42	8:31:00

Women

Year	Name	Swimming	Cycling	Running	Totals
1979	Lyn Lemaire	1:16:20	6:30	5:10	12:55:38
1980	Robin Beck	1:20	6:05	3:56:24	11:21:24
1981	Linda Sweeney	1:02:07	6:53:28	4:04:57	12:00:32
1982 (Feb)	Kathleen McCartney	1:32	5:51:12	3:46:28	11:09:40
1982 (Oct)	Julie Leach	1:04:57	5:50:36	3:58:35	10:54:08
1983	Sylviane Puntous	1:00:28	6:20:40	3:22:28	10:43:36
1984	Sylviane Puntous	1:00:45.2	5:50:36.7	3:33:51.4	10:25:13.3
1985	Joanne Ernst	1:01:43	5:39:13	3:44:26	10:25:22
1986	Paula Newbury-Fraser	0:57:03.1	5:32:05.6	3:20:05.7	9:49:14.5
1987	Erin Baker	0:57:42	5:26:34	3:11:08	9:35:25
1988	Paula Newbury-Fraser	0:56:38	4:57:13	3:07:09	9:01:01

Alexandra Kremer – Germany's best woman triathlete of recent years.

Winners of the World Championships at Nice

Year	Name	Totals
1982	Mark Allen Lyn Brooks	6:33:52 7:40:44
1983	Mark Allen Linda Buchanan	6:04:51 7:06:03
1984	Mark Allen Colleen Cannon	6:05:22 7:05:15
1985	Mark Allen Erin Baker	5:53:13 6:37:21
1986	Mark Allen Linda Buchanan	5:46:10 6:50:56
1987	Rick Wells Kirstie Hanssen	5:59:53 6:54:27
1988	Rob Barel Erin Baker	6:05:06 6:27:06

Winners of the official European Championships 1985

Triathlon relay: (Belfast/ Northern Ireland)	Dutch team (Barel, Hellemans, Huls, Koenders)
Short triathlon: 1.3/60/12.3 (Immenstadt/ West Germany)	Rob Barel (NL) 2:37:42 Alexandra Kremer (WG) 3:06:02
Middle triathlon: 1.9/90/21.1 (Aabenraa/ Denmark)	Peter Ziyerveld (NL) 4:10:05 Lieve Paulus (Bel) 4:45:19
Long triathlon: 2.4/180/42 (Almere/ Netherlands)	Gregor Stam (NL) 8:56:55 Sarah Springman (GB) 10:18:53

Winners of the official European Championships 1986

Triathlon relay: (Mansfield/ Great Britain)	West German team (Kremer, Rupp, Wachter, Zäck)
Short triathlon: 1/44/12 (Milton Keynes/ Great Britain)	Rob Barel (NL) 1:59:50 Lieve Paulus (Bel) 2:17:10
Middle triathlon: 1.9/90/21 (Brasschaat/ Belgium)	Rob Barel (NL) 3:54:31 Sarah Coope (GB) 4:32:13
Long triathlon: 3.8/180/42 (Säter/Sweden)	Magnus Lönnquist (Fin) 8:40:11 Sarah Springman (GB) 9:59:49

Winners of the official European Championships 1987

Short triathlon: 1/45/10 (Marseille/ France)	Rob Barel (NL) 1:58:12 Sarah Coope (GB) 2:17:02
Middle triathlon: 2/92/20 (Roth/ West Germany)	Glenn Cook (GB) 3:57:19 Sarah Coope (GB) 4:28:38
Long triathlon: 3.8/180/42 (Joroinen/ Finland)	Axel Koenders (NL) 8:36:22 Sarah Coope (GB) 9:48:17

Winners of the official European Championships 1988

Short triathlon:	no championship
Middle triathlon:	Rob Barel (NL) Sarah Coope (GB)
Long triathlon:	no championship

Winners of the British Championships

1985		
Short course:	Peter Moysey Sarah Springman	
Long course:	Mark Knagg Sarah Springman	
1986		
Short course:	Glenn Cook Sarah Springman	
Long course:	Glenn Cook Sarah Springman	
1987		
Short course:	Mike Harris Sarah Springman	
Long course:	Glenn Cook Sarah Springman	
1988		
Short course:	Mark Marabini Sarah Springman	
Long course:	Mark Marabini Sarah Springman	

Triathlon series

Apart from the official championships, most of the leading triathlon nations hold triathlon series. These are a series of separate events that are held throughout the season at various locations. The overall series winner is worked out by means of a points system at the end of the season.

The distances are usually relatively short at such events. The best-known series is the *USTS* or *United States Triathlon Series.* Here the distances have been fixed since 1984 at 1.5 km swimming, 40 km cycling and 10 km running. This is to ensure the fairest ratio between the constituent disciplines.

In 1985 the first *British Grand Prix Series* took place, and has continued ever since, though with changes in the method of scoring. These events were heavily over-subscribed.

Glenn Cook, European Half Ironman Champion in 1987.

Nottingham. The running and cycling sections took place along the interior perimeter road around the city centre.

Junior Championships have been held in Great Britain every year since, but the overall response from juniors has been disappointing – particularly when so much progress is being made in other European countries such as France and Germany.

The triathlon is ideal for young athletes provided the correct programme is followed.

People's triathlon

One recent development is the people's triathlon, which is based on the same principle as people's marathons and cycle touring events. The distances are less than those for even the short triathlon. But the event is nonetheless a continuous one, with no breaks between the constituent elements of swimming, cycling and running. The overall time is calculated for each competitor, who is issued with a certificate showing what he or she has achieved. Participants don't have to belong to any sports association, and may try out the course beforehand to see if they can manage it. A subscription is payable to cover the expenses incurred by the organising body, including insurance for those taking part.

Typical lengths:

	Swimming	Cycling	Running
Beginners	300 m	5 km	1.7 – 2.0 km
Experienced	700 m	10 – 12 km	5.0 – 6.0 km

Youth events

In 1985 a *British Junior Championship* was organised using the National Water Sports Centre at Holmepierrepont,

Multiple endurance competitions

There is a tradition of multiple endurance competitions that comes outside the category of the triathlon proper. Each of these competitions is made up of several different endurance tests, either on a single day or spread out over a specific period. Each part is assessed on its own, and the results are then added together to give an overall winner. Unlike in the triathlon, there are rest intervals between each part, though their length varies from one competition to another.

The Swedish Classic
Begun in 1970, this is the longest established of the multiple endurance competitions, and also the most demanding. The following elements must be completed within the course of a year: the Wasa Race – an 89 km cycle race around the shores of Lake Vättern; the 30 km Lindigo Run; and the 3 km Vansbro River Swim. There are thousands of enthusiastic participants every year.

The Norwegian Classic
The Norwegian version was introduced in 1974. The constituent events are as follows: 42 km of cross-country skiing from Holmenkollen to Marsjen; 170 km of cycling from Holnsvannet to Rundt; and a 20 km cross-country run from Fredrikstadmarka to Rundt.

The German Classic
The Husum Tetrathlon was started in 1976. It is made up of four events that take place within a single week during the summer: a 50 km walk, a 1.5 km swim, a 150 km cycle run and a marathon run.

Swimming

The basic requirements for swimming training are **swimming trunks** or a **swimming costume,** a **bathing cap** and **goggles.** The goggles are needed to protect the eyes against chemicals such as chlorine in the swimming baths or the salt in sea water. Prolonged exposure to these during training can lead to redness and inflammation of the mucous membranes just inside the eyelids.

The choice of goggles will depend on individual preference. It is best to try out a variety of makes and models before deciding on which kind to buy. It is important to stop the lenses misting up. Often all you need to do is to rub some spittle over them or rinse them with a little

hair shampoo. Anti-fog goggles will have been specially treated to prevent them misting up.

One-piece triathlon suit.

A **nose peg** and **ear plugs** are only needed if you are allergic to chlorine, or if you don't like water getting into your nose and ear passages.

A **one-piece triathlon suit** is worn for all three parts of a triathlon competition, so that no change of costume is required. Such a suit is made of a quick-drying material, and is designed to cling to the body without restricting movement.

Neoprene suits have been specially developed for the triathlon, and can be worn in water of any temperature. Neoprene is a kind of artificial rubber that stretches easily and provides good insulation against the cold. This is because of the thousands of tiny air bubbles that are trapped inside it. The air conducts heat much less well than water, and so prevents body heat from escaping. The material also prevents water from getting inside the costume and allowing heat to escape.

Neoprene suits vary in thickness from 1.5 mm to 3 mm, and come in both long-sleeved and sleeveless varieties. They allow you to stay in cold water for some considerable time without risk of getting chilled, because the body, upper thighs and neck in particular are insulated against the cold. The soft inner lining makes them comfortable to wear and easy to get in or out of. An exact fit is needed in order to get the full benefit of a neoprene suit. If it is too big it will let water in, allowing heat to escape. If it is

Swimming checklist:

Swimming trunks/costume
Bathing cap
Swim goggles
Nose peg/ear plugs
Triathlon suit
Neoprene suit and cap
Vaseline
Pullbuoy
Float
Swim paddles
Waterproof watch

too tight, this restricts blood circulation under the skin.

A large amount of heat is lost through the head during swimming, so cold-water swimmers are advised to wear a **neoprene cap** too. The extra warmth also enables you to conserve energy, which can be harnessed towards swimming faster. **Vaseline** can be used to prevent the neoprene suit rubbing in areas such as the neck and shoulders.

The training aids that are most frequently used by swimmers are the pullbuoy, the float and swim paddles. A **pullbuoy** should be gripped between the thighs so as to hold the body horizontal when you are concentrating on armstroke technique. The **float** has a long history of success as an aid to learning or improving the leg stroke in the

Neoprene suits – short and long.

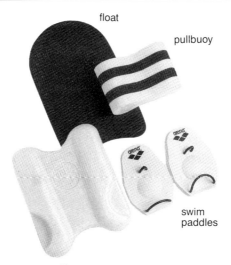

float

pullbuoy

swim paddles

pullbuoy

crawl. Thus it is useful for both beginners and experts alike.

Swim paddles are made of plastic, and are fixed to the hands by means of elastic bands. Because they increase the effective surface area of the hands, more strength is needed to swim with them. Thus they help to develop the arm muscles (see also strength endurance training). Swim paddles are available in different sizes, and can also be used for improving armstroke technique. This is because the increased water resistance tends to highlight any faults in the arm movements during the underwater phase.

A **waterproof watch** is another vital addition to the triathlete's armoury. It enables you to monitor your own performance during training, in particular during interval training and time trials. It is also useful in competitions, because knowing the time means that you can pace yourself better in relation to your strength reserves.

Cycling

The conventional road-racing bike has been the standard form used in the triathlon, and until recently was considered entirely adequate for both training and competition. But more recent research suggests that the special circumstances of the triathlon require a machine that is specifically adapted. The road-racing bike was never intended for a cyclist who is racing alone without the benefit of slipstreaming.

This realisation has led to some interesting experimentation among top international triathletes. Aerodynamic design has become increasingly important so as to reduce wind resistance to the minimum. At the 1986 German Championships at Roth, Scott Tinley

The components of a road-racing bike:

The frame.

The steering, including handlbars and stem, headset and forks.

The transmission, consisting of bottom bracket (including bearings, cranks and chainwheels), pedals, freewheel sprockets, gears and chain.

The wheels, consisting of hubs, spokes and rims.

The tyres.

The braking system.

The saddle and seat stem.

Accessories such as type pump, spare tyre, bottle in bottle holder, odometer and other measuring devices, and mudguards for wet weather.

made his appearance on a new high-tech racing model that was specially suited to the requirements of the short, middle and long triathlons. It weighed only 8.5 kg, thanks to its carbon-fibre frame. The handlebars were fully streamlined, as were the spokes, of which there was the minimum possible number.

Views differ as to the best bicycle design for the triathlon. Some people favour a time-trial model, with a sloping top tube, a 24-inch or 26-inch front wheel and a covered wheel design. Others prefer a machine with disc-type wheels made of aluminium or carbon fibre, buffalo handlebars, and other refinements such as brake cables enclosed in the frame.

It is up to individual triathletes to choose or construct the kind of model that best suits their own specific aims and requirements. An ordinary touring bike is quite sufficient for the people's triathlon, whereas top performers will need to take account of small details such as frame size and saddle position. These must be adjusted exactly to suit the triathlete's own height and build if the best possible performance is to be achieved.

The frame

This is the most important part of a racing bike. It must be as light as possible, but sufficiently stable at the same time. This is to ensure the optimum transfer of power from the legs to the wheels. At a riding speed of 35–42 km/h (22–26 mph), each extra kilo in weight means an increase in effort of up to two per cent. But if the frame is too light, valuable energy is wasted as the frame sags under the weight of the body.

Frames are usually made of a manganese or chrome-molybdenum

A modern time-trial bike, suitable for using in the triathlon.

The frame of a racing bicycle.

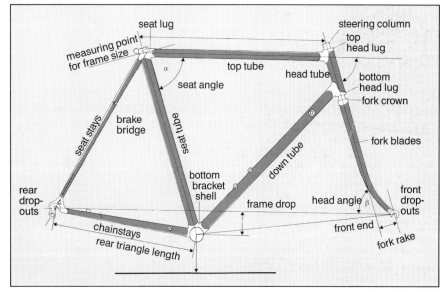

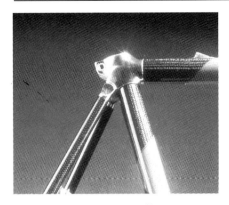

A carbon frame, showing the fibre structure.

alloy steel, both for the triathlon and for cycling generally. Reynolds tubes, being the most stable, are the ones used by French, Dutch and English manufacturers. But the Italians prefer Columbus tubes, which are lighter but correspondingly less stable. Really good frames are normally hand-made, and weigh about 2.5 kg.

There have recently been advances in the manufacture of light, aerodynamic frames made of carbon fibre or aluminium. A carbon frame has been developed weighing only 1.7 kg, which is about as light as one could possibly go. Such innovations may open new horizons to women athletes and lightweight males. Light frames, however, are not suited to heavier riders, because any weight advantages are cancelled out by the loss of power that results from a sagging frame.

There are advantages in having a frame with a top tube that slopes down towards the front. This is because the body position is more streamlined as a result. Such designs are on the increase – and not only in the triathlon, because they work so much better generally, both

on the flat and when riding against the wind.

Frame size and top tube length

These are the two most important dimensions of a bicycle frame. Both must be adapted to suit the triathlete's height and build.

Frame size is given in centimetres, and is normally measured from the centre of the bottom bracket to the top edge of the seat tube. However, there are a few manufacturers who measure from the centre of the bottom bracket to the centre of the top tube. These two measurements differ by about 0.5 cm. So

if in doubt, measure the frame size for yourself!

There are several different ways of determining the correct frame size for a particular rider. Leg height, stride length and body height may all be taken into account, but body height is the least accurate guide.

If a frame is made to measure, the **top tube length** can also be adjusted to suit individual requirements. The two main criteria in this case are the torso length (measured from the thigh bone to the shoulder), and the arm length (measured from the wrist to the shoulder) both of which should be added together.

Frame size in relation to leg height, stride length and body height

Frame Size (cm)	Leg height (cm)	Stride length (cm)	Body height (cm)
51.0	80.0	76.0	
51.5	81.0	76.5	
52.0	81.5	77.0	160 – 165
52.5	82.0	77.5	
53.0	83.0	78.0	
53.5	84.0	78.5	
54.0	84.5	79.0	
54.5	85.0	79.5	165 – 170
55.0	86.0	80.0	
55.5	87.0	80.5	
56.0	88.0	81.0	
56.5	89.0	81.5	170 – 175
57.0	89.5	82.0	
57.5	90.0	82.5	
58.0	91.0	83.0	175 – 180
58.5	92.0	83.5	
59.0	93.0	84.0	180 – 185
59.5	94.0	84.5	
60.0	95.0	85.0	185 – 190
60.5	96.0	85.5	
61.0	97.0	86.0	
61.5	98.0	86.5	over 190
61.5	99.0	86.5	
62.0	100.0	87.0	

Top tube length in relation to torso length plus arm length

Torso length plus arm length (cm)	Top tube length (cm)
100	53.0
101	53.4
102	53.8
103	54.1
104	54.4
105	54.7
106	55.0
107	55.3
108	55.6
109	55.9
110	56.2
111	56.5
112	56.8
113	57.1
114	57.4
115	57.7
116	58.0
117	58.3
118	58.6
119	58.0
120	59.0
121	59.2
122	59.4
123	59.6
124	59.8
125	60.0

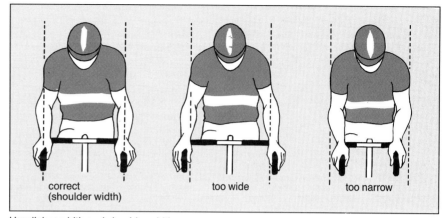

Handlebar width and shoulder width.

correct distance between the bars and the saddle. When the frame is not made to measure, the top tube length may be incompatible with the torso and arm lengths (see above), but this anomaly can be rectified by adjusting the handlebar stem. Stems vary in length from 6 cm to 14 cm, and the angle varies according to type. The sprint and track types ensure that the body position is well streamlined.

The **handlebar shape** also varies enormously. The choice of model will depend very much on the preferred hand position in training and/or competition (see also **Riding posture** on page 46), and on the individual triathlete's own personal goals. A more all-round competitor should opt for the normal road bars. A top performer, on the other hand, will need the advantages provided by the more aerodynamically designed models

The steering

The steering system is made up of handlebars and stem, headset and forks. The **handlebars** and **stem** are usually made of duralumin. Like the frame, they are available in different sizes. **Handlebar width** should be determined according to shoulder width, and may vary from 38 cm to 44.5 cm. The bars are measured from the centre of the tube at either end.

The dimensions of the **handlebar stem** should be chosen to ensure the

Different types of handlebar stem.

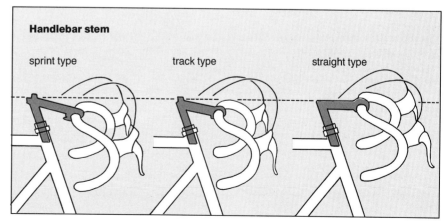

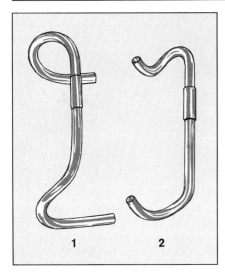

Different types of bars:

1 Road bars – Tour de France or Giro d'Italia, depending on the manufacturer.
2 Horn or buffalo bars.

such as the horn or buffalo bars, which are becoming increasingly popular in the triathlon. Scott Tinley has his bars specially designed – a possible pointer to the future development of special triathlon bars.

The **headset** is the name for the bearings that secure both the forks and the handlebar stem in the head tube of the frame. Headsets are made variously of steel, duralumin or titanium. The last two are noticeably lighter, but are also more expensive. The headset should be carefully adjusted so that the bars and forks turn easily without any play.

The handling of the bike depends very much on the angle and rake of the **forks.** If the forks are straighter and more upright, then less energy is lost on hills, when the climbing position is used (see page 49). But such forks are only suited to good road conditions, because they cope less well with rough surfaces.

The transmission

The chainset

The chainset consists of bottom bracket axle and bearings, cranks and chainwheels, together with the various screwed fittings that hold them together. All the parts should be of the same make (Campagnolo, Shimano or whatever) so that they will fit together properly. The chainset is made of high-quality materials, duralumin or titanium being lighter but more expensive. It should always be kept in immaculate condition, because it is the point where the transmission begins.

The **cranks** should be measured from the centre of the bottom bracket axle to the pedal spindle. The correct length will depend on the rider's leg

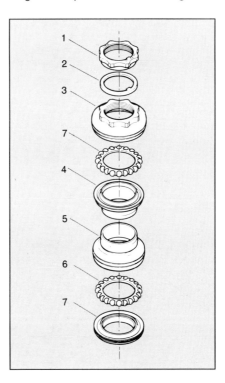

height and stride length. The longer the cranks, the greater the leverage and the more efficient the transmission (an advantage on hills), but the more power is needed to turn the pedals.

The exact choice of **chainwheels** will depend both on the difficulty of the course and on the triathlete's level of attainment. The small chainwheel normally has 42 teeth, the large one 52 or 53 (see also page 24). Shimano have recently devised a chainwheel called Biopace that is specially suited to the triathlon. It has been biomechanically designed using computer simulation methods so as to make the pedals work as efficiently as possible. The chainwheel is oval in shape, so more power is required when the cranks are horizontal and less when they are vertical. It remains to be seen whether this innovation will catch on in practice.

Guide to crank size

Frame size (cm)	Crank size (mm)
50 – 55	170
56 – 59	170 – 172.5
60 – 61	172.5 – 175

Pedals

The traditional racing pedals with toeclips and straps are gradually giving way to a safety pedal developed by Look. This new system was first used successfully by professional cyclists in the 1986 Tour de France.

The headset consists of the following parts:

1 locknut
2 lock washer
3 screwed race
4 top head race
5 bottom head race
6 crown race
7 caged bearings.

A safety pedal with the appropriate shoeplate.

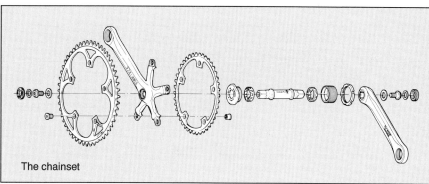

The chainset

The safety pedal allows the shoe to be engaged or removed by means of a device similar to ski bindings. The shoe is firmly attached to the pedal, ensuring the efficient transfer of power. But a quick sideways movement allows the shoe to be speedily removed for dismounting, whatever the position of the cranks. This means the rider can stop more easily in dangerous situations – a desirable safety feature for triathletes competing at all levels. The shoe can also be left attached to the pedal so as to save time at the change-over, because a triathlete can then mount the bike and put on his shoes in a single manoeuvre.

For those who prefer pedals with **toeclips,** it is important to match the toeclip size to the shoe size. When the ball of the foot is placed over the pedal

spindle, there should be about 2 mm space between the front of the toeclip and the end of the shoe.

Shoeplates should not be attached to new shoes until they have been used a few times. The pedals will then leave marks on the soles of the shoes, which will indicate where the shoeplates are to be mounted. (The pedalling technique must be clean and correct to ensure the accuracy of this method.) If shoeplates are wrongly positioned, this will make the pedalling less effective and may

An oval-shaped chainwheel works like this. When the crank is at the top (the "dead point") of the circle, the chainwheel radius is greater and the pedalling power is increased. The radius is then reduced (right) when the cranks are horizontal and less pedalling power is required.

eventually lead to knee and ankle problems.

The freewheel
The freewheel sprockets are either screwed onto the hub (screwed freewheel) or else splined to it using a cassette system (cassette hub and freewheel). Freewheels are usually made of steel. Duralumin or titanium models are lighter but more expensive. Triathletes normally use freewheels with six or seven sprockets. The sprockets can be replaced individually.

Derailleur gears
This is the normal type of gear system used on racing bikes. It consists of two main mechanisms: the **front changer** is operated by the left gear lever, and moves the chain between the small

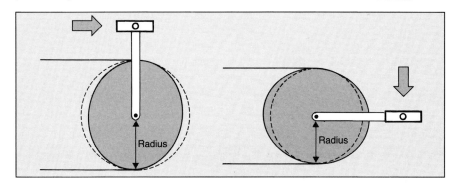

Toeclips in relation to shoe size

Shoe size	Type of toeclip	Size of toeclip	Shoe size	Insertion depth of shoe
37	small toeclip	7.5 cm	37	10.0 – 10.5 cm
38		7.5 cm	38	10.5 – 11.0 cm
39		7.5 cm	39	11.0 – 11.5 cm
40	medium toeclip	8.5 cm	40	11.5 – 12.0 cm
41		8.5 cm	41	12.0 – 12.5 cm
42		8.5 cm	42	12.5 – 13.0 cm
43		9.5 cm	43	13.0 – 13.5 cm
44	large toeclip	9.5 cm	44	13.5 – 14.0 cm
45		9.5 cm	45	14.0 – 14.5 cm
46		9.5 cm	46	14.5 – 15.0 cm

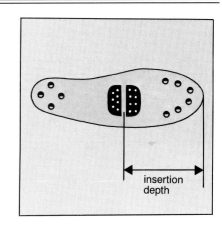

insertion depth

chainwheel and the large one; the **rear derailleur** is operated by the right gear lever, and moves the chain across the sprockets of the freewheel.

A good gear system should be able to cope with chainwheels that differ by as many as twelve teeth (eg 42/54), and a freewheel with a difference of 14 or 15 teeth between the smallest and largest sprocket (eg 12–26). Changing gear used to be a delicate procedure involving a considerable amount of skill, but it has become much easier since the advent of the SIS gear system. Even more experienced riders can change gear more frequently with an SIS system, making the pedalling more even and efficient.

The chain

A racing chain is narrow (1/2″ × 3/32″) and is made up of an average of 108 links. The chain length should be checked by laying the chain over the largest chainwheel and sprocket. In this position it should be held straight without being under tension.

The ideal **chainline** lies parallel to the centre line of the frame. The further away from this line the chain is, the more energy is lost through the friction that is produced between the links. So it is important not to use gears that use the largest sprocket with the smaller chainwheel, or conversely the smallest sprocket with the larger chainwheel.

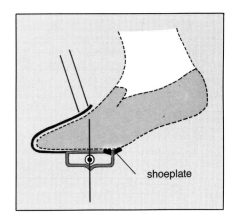

shoeplate

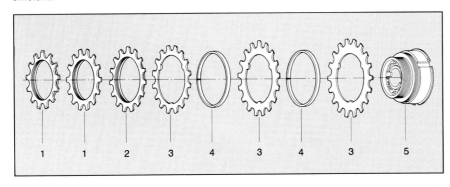

Screwed freewheel:
1 2 3 sprockets
4 spacers
5 freewheel body.

The wheels

A wheel consists of a rim and a hub connected by spokes. Lightness isn't the only prerequisite for a good **rim,** which must also be sufficiently sturdy. Rims for tubular tyres are normally up to 22 mm wide and weigh 300–450 g. Rims for wired tyres are rather heavier, but have the same diameter (27″). The development of aerodynamically designed rims is of particular interest to triathletes. Such rims have a triangular cross-section, with the spokes emerging from the apex of the triangle.

The **hubs** are subjected to a lot of physical pressures, and their quality determines the smoothness with which the wheel turns. So it is important not to skimp on hubs, and to go for well-established makes. Hubs should be fitted with a quick-release mechanism that allows the wheels to be changed quickly.

A covered wheel.

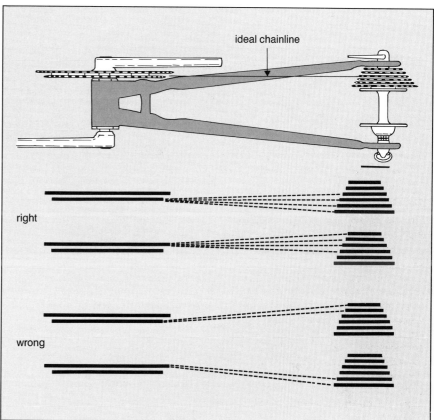

Right and wrong gear combinations in relation to the chainline.

Ordinary wheels have 36 **spokes.** But triathletes often use rims with 32, 28 or even 24 spokes so as to reduce turbulence and the consequent drag. For the same reason the spoking is often radial (whereas ordinary wheels have crossed spoking, crossing three or crossing four, to make the wheel more elastic). A radially spoked front wheel with 36 spokes and a streamlined rim has the same aerodynamic qualities as a 28-spoke wheel with an ordinary rim.

A wheel with fewer spokes is of course more easily damaged in a crash, and being less sturdy is unsuitable for heavy riders. Large-flange hubs are needed for rims with fewer than 32 spokes. The larger flange means shorter spokes, and the wheel is given the necessary stability. Flattened spokes are better aerodynamically, but are very expensive, and are only recommended for high-performance triathletes.

Disc-type wheels made of aluminium or carbon fibre are even better

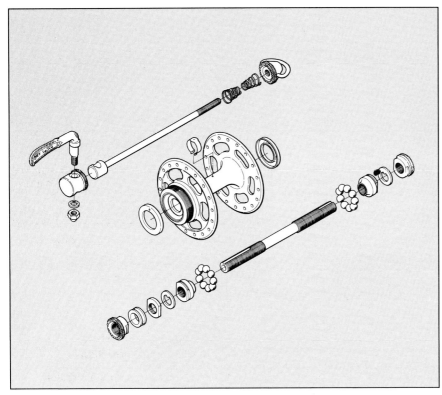

Hub and quick-release mechanism.

aerodynamically, as Francesco Moser demonstrated in his famous world record attempts. But they cost at least £300 and sometimes over £1,000, so are well beyond the reach of most ordinary people.

Covered wheels have similar aerodynamic advantages in that there is no turbulence around the spokes. These are spoked wheels to which covers have been attached. The covers are relatively light, and cost anything from about £100. They will benefit any triathlete who achieves an average of 33–36 km/h over a distance of 50 km. The speed gains are even more noticeable at higher speeds.

The tyres

The first choice that needs to be made is between ordinary wired tyres and tubular racing tyres. An **ordinary tyre** consists of an inner tube and a separate outer cover. The beading along the edges of the cover has wire running through it. This is pressed against the rim when the tube is inflated, thus securing the tyre in the rim.

In a **tubular tyre,** the tube is sewn into the cotton or silk carcass of the cover. Thus the tube is integral with the cover. Tubular tyres must be stuck to the rim using rim cement or double-sided rim tape. This job must be done with great

care so as to ensure that the tyre doesn't suddenly come away from the rim under extreme pressure, such as when turning sharply at speed.

Ordinary tyres or tubulars?

A good tyre must have the following characteristics in order to cope with the special demands of the triathlon:

- light in weight
- not liable to punctures
- good road-holding
- low friction and drag
- long-lasting
- easy to repair or change if punctured during training or competition.

In order to assess these points, one must first be familiar with some basic physical concepts.

Rolling resistance or **friction** is produced by the contact between the tyre and the road or track surface. It is not affected by the rider's technique, but by the characteristics of the two surfaces in contact. The amount of resistance can be expressed using the following formula:

$$F_R = F_N \times \frac{f}{r}$$

F_R = the force equivalent to the rolling resistance.

F_N = the force equivalent to the weight of the triathlete and his bike perpendicular to the road surface.

f = the distance between the theoretical contact point and the actual point at which the tyre first touches the road surface.

r = the radius of the wheels (half the normal diameter of 27″).

The following conditions must be met in order to reduce resistance (F_R) to a minimum: firstly, the bike and rider must weigh as little as possible (F_N); and secondly, the contact area between the tyre and the road (f) must be kept to a minimum.

The contact area is the same for all tyres with the same pressure, whatever their width. So an expensive narrow tyre is no advantage if the pressure is too low; on the contrary, it is more liable to puncture. On the other hand, if the pressure is too high there are other problems, such as the tendency to skid on bends or over wet surfaces.

Ordinary tyres must never be inflated beyond the prescribed pressure (up to seven atmospheres), otherwise the wires may become overstretched and slip out over the rim. So if you want to pump the tyres up very hard to reduce rolling resistance, you must always opt for tubular tyres.

As the wheels turn the tyres are compressed and deformed at the point where they come into contact with the road. This compression uses up energy. The more easily a tyre is compressed, the less energy is lost and the more energy is left to overcome rolling resistance. Tests have shown that lighter tyres, being more flexible, use up less energy as they are compressed. And tubular tyres are always the lightest.

A tyre must also have good **road-holding** characteristics. The width makes no difference here, and it is wrong to imagine that wide tyres grip better than narrow ones. The important factor is the road-holding characteristics of the tread. A soft tread holds the road better, but also wears out more quickly. A hard tread lasts longer, but holds the road less well. However, tyres rarely run to their full lifespan, so the advantages of a soft tread probably outweigh the disadvantages. The best choice are the so-called "slick" tyres that are already smooth when you buy them.

The amount of rolling resistance depends on how much of the tyre is in contact with the road:

1 Sufficient tyre pressure and a good road surface mean that the contact area is small and the amount of resistance is correspondingly small.
2 A bad road surface, combined with insufficient tyre pressure, means a large contact area and hence a considerable amount of resistance.
3 The road surface is good, but the tyre pressure is not high enough. The result is increased resistance due to the greater contact area.

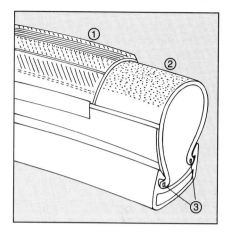

The structure of an ordinary wired tyre:

1 Rubber covering or tread.
2 Cotton carcass.
3 Beading with a wire inlay.

The structure of a tubular tyre:

1 Tread made of natural rubber.
2 Cotton carcass.
3 Polyurethane layer to protect against damage.
4 Butyl tube.
5 Chafing tape to protect the stitching.
6 Rim.

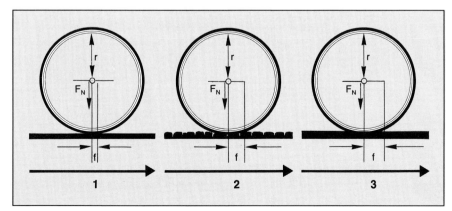

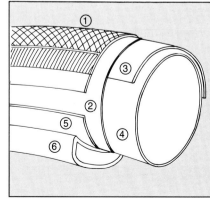

Ordinary tyres are sturdier and less liable to **puncture** than tubulars. They are also cheaper and easier to repair. Depending on the make, they tend to be narrower than tubulars, and this means less **drag** or wind resistance. A tubular can be more quickly changed during training or competition, but only if you cut corners with the sticking process, running the risk that the tyre may come away from the rim.

The fragility of a tubular tyre can be reduced by "maturing" it over a long period. A fresh new tyre is very easily punctured because the tread is too soft, and sharp stones or pieces of glass can easily get embedded in the tread. So it is

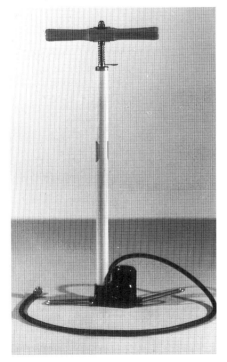

A track pump with a pressure gauge.

a good idea to keep a tyre for a year or two, or even longer if possible, so as to allow the tread to harden before it is mounted on the wheel.

Triathletes nowadays tend to opt for a tyre that is slightly heavier but with a protective layer that helps guard against punctures. Examples of this are Panarecer Tour Guard (both wired and tubular tyres), Wolber Invulnerable, Mutan Kevlar and Michelin BIB TS (wired tyres only).

Track pump

A track pump with a pressure gauge is essential in order to obtain the ideal tyre pressure in individual situations. The correct tyre pressure will depend on the type of tyre (ordinary or tubular), the weight of the rider and the riding conditions. Ordinary tyres and tubulars for training can be pumped up to between five and seven atmospheres. Good tubulars for competitions can stand eight atmospheres or more. If the tyres are pumped up too hard, they will grip less well on bends and over wet surfaces.

The brakes

Racing bikes are fitted with either side-pull or centre-pull brakes. **Side-pull brakes** have a sharper braking effect, but need more frequent adjustment because the cable pulls on the side of the mechanism. **Centre-pull brakes** work more evenly but are also less powerful. The cables pull on the centre of the mechanism. Centre-pull brakes have been considerably improved in recent years, and are being used increasingly in the triathlon.

The aerodynamics are improved if the **brake cables** are mounted inside the frame.

The **brake levers** are mounted on

Conventional side-pull brakes.

the handlebars in such a way that they can always be reached easily, whether from above (on the hoods) or below (on the drops).

Good brakes are equipped with a quick-release mechanism. This not only makes it much easier to change a wheel quickly, but it also means that a rider can carry on if a wheel is buckled in an accident.

The saddle

At one time **leather saddles** were the only kind used. They are very hard when new; they must be gradually "broken in" and softened over a period, and regularly restretched. They require a lot of care and attention, especially after riding through rain, in order to keep their shape and to keep the leather supple. Their weight is also a disadvantage, being about 600 g.

Modern **plastic saddles** are much lighter (about 200–350 g); they need less care, and no "breaking in" is required. The plastic shell is lightly padded and covered with suede or soft leather. Suede is less slippery, but wears out more quickly.

The **seat pillar** must fit exactly into the seat tube of the frame, which may vary in diameter from 25 mm to 27.4 mm. It must be inserted at least 6 cm into the seat tube. It is normally between 13 cm and 18 cm long. If it is too long, there will be unnecessary extra weight to carry.

Accessories

Tyre pump

Spare tyres
One or two tubulars or tubes for ordinary tyres. They can be folded up small, and should be kept in a bag to prevent them getting wet or rubbing against the saddle.

Drinking bottle and cage
An aerodynamically designed bottle is an advantage in the triathlon. This means, however, that the rider must fend for himself over long distances, because race organisers normally only provide the traditional round bottles.

Odometer
The rapid advances in microcomputer technology have created a wide choice of sophisticated odometers providing all kinds of useful information. They are particularly helpful for checking performance, both in training and competition. Most models incorporate the following functions:

- average speed
- maximum speed
- total distance
- day's distance
- stopwatch

Some odometers can even be linked to special equipment for measuring

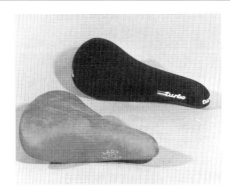

Types of racing saddle – in front a so-called lady's saddle.

pedalling speed and pulse rate. Odometers are usually mounted on the handlebars or front forks.

Mudguards
These are needed in wet weather to protect both rider and machine from the water that is thrown up by the tyres.

CO2 cartridges
These small cartridges filled with carbon dioxide are a marvellous time- and energy-saving device. They can be used after a puncture in a race to pump up a tyre quickly and without effort to over six atmospheres.

The right saddle position

All triathletes should try to work out the exact saddle position that enables them to perform at their own personal best. This applies as much to all-round performers as to top triathletes. Why should unnecessary energy be wasted, simply because you are continually having to correct your hand position or shift uncomfortably around the saddle?

Several measurements should already have been worked out before you

go on to check the saddle position. You should have already obtained a bicycle with the correct frame size, top tube length and crank length for you. Handlebars and toeclips should also have been matched to your dimensions.

Saddle height
This is first important measurement to be worked out. There are three possible tests for checking to see if this is correct. They should be carried out with the pedal at the lowest point in the circle, and preferably with racing shoes on, as the thickness of the sole will be enough to make a difference to the result obtained. The three procedures are as follows:

- Place the ball of the foot on the pedal. Your leg should be not quite straight, with the knee forming an angle of 130–175° (see below).
- Place your heel on the pedal. Your leg should now be completely straight (see overleaf top left).
- Put your toes underneath the pedal so that the sole of the foot is parallel to the ground. Your leg should again be straight (see overleaf top centre).

The leg position when the saddle is at the correct height.

When your leg is straight, you must be able to reach the pedal with your heel.

When your leg is straight, you must be able to get your toes under the pedal.

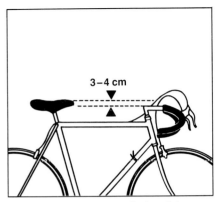

3–4 cm

Saddle height in relation to the handlebar stem.

When the saddle is in the correct position, the seat pillar should not protrude more than 8–11 cm out of the seat tube. If it does, then the frame size is wrong.

Saddle angle
This should be worked out using a spirit level or a long broom handle to check that the saddle is both horizontal and parallel to the top tube.

If the saddle position is correct, the front knee should be vertically above the pedal axle when the cranks are horizontal.

Saddle position
There are two ways of working out the correct horizontal position of the saddle:

- If a plumb-line is dropped from the front point of the saddle, it should fall 2–5 cm behind the centre of the bottom bracket axle.
- Adopt your riding position with the cranks placed horizontally. A plumb-line dropped from the front point of the forward knee should fall through the pedal axle (see bottom left).

The saddle can be moved forwards or backwards on the seat pillar to adjust.

Reach
This is the distance from the back of the saddle to the nearest part of the handlebars. It can be corrected by adjusting the handlebar stem. Again there are two ways of checking the reach:

- Place your elbow at the front point of the saddle. Your outstretched fingers should touch the handlebar stem about 3 cm behind the bars.
- Adopt your riding position with your hands on the drops and the cranks running parallel to the down tube. Your elbow should just touch your knee on one side (see bottom centre).

If you need a handlebar stem longer than 14 cm, this means the top tube length is too short. The handlebars and stem should be positioned 3–4 cm below the saddle (see top right).

If the handlebar stem is at the correct height, the knee and elbow may just touch as shown in the picture, with the hands on the drops and the cranks parallel to the down tube.

Measurement chart

Once you have worked out your ideal saddle position on your bike, you should note down the measurements carefully on a chart (see bottom right) so that you can reproduce the same position on a new bike. Then you will find that your technique and position are completely unaffected when you change your bike.

Bicycle maintenance

However well you prepare yourself for a competition, all your efforts will be in vain if you are badly placed or forced to drop out, simply because something is wrong with your bike that you could have prevented. Regular care and maintenance of equipment is just as much part of the triathlon as systematic training in the three sporting disciplines.

Cleaning the bike

This is particularly important after riding in the rain, or in the winter when there is salt on the roads. You will need the following items for the purpose:

- a bucket of water with a little detergent
- a bottle of diesel oil
- a sponge
- a soft brush
- a large paintbrush or an old toothbrush
- chrome polish

The wheels should be cleaned with the sponge and the tyres with the soft brush. If the chain is very dirty, it should be wiped with the paintbrush dipped in diesel oil before you start the bike wash proper. Diesel should similarly be used to clean the brakes and the gears (including the front changer, rear derailleur and freewheel). No water should be allowed to get into these parts while the bike is being washed. Once the bike is clean

and dry, you should give another dose of oil to the chain and all the moving parts of the gears and brakes.

Every now and then some chrome polish should be applied to the handlebar stem, seat pillar, brakes, hubs, spokes and rims – and also to the cranks, the chainwheels and finally the pedals.

The chief maintenance jobs

One of the most important jobs is replacing the chain. This is necessary if more than three or four chainlinks can be lifted off the large chainwheel at one time (see top left overleaf). Brake blocks must always be replaced if they are worn out. The brake cables should be regularly checked and if necessary replaced.

Once a year the hubs should be dismantled, cleaned and regreased – and similarly the handlebar stem and seat pillar. Every now and then the cranks should be tightened using a special spanner, and the headset should be checked for any play. If the headset is worn it should be replaced.

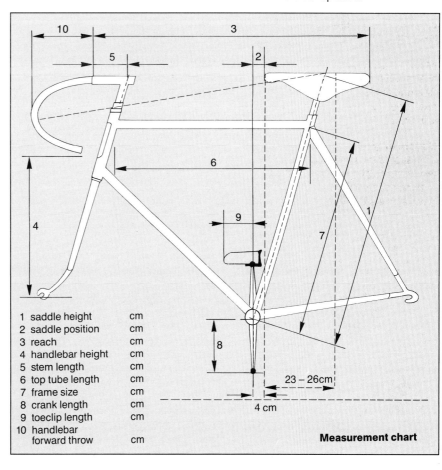

1	saddle height	cm
2	saddle position	cm
3	reach	cm
4	handlebar height	cm
5	stem length	cm
6	top tube length	cm
7	frame size	cm
8	crank length	cm
9	toeclip length	cm
10	handlebar forward throw	cm

Measurement chart

Checking the chain tension.

Trueing a wheel.

The wheels should be carefully trued after training rides on poor surfaces, before competitions, or after the first ride on newly spoked wheels. Buckles can be corrected using a nipple key (see top centre). If the rim is buckled to the right, then the right spokes should be loosened and the left spokes tightened along the part of the rim that is affected. Turn the nipple key to the left (anticlockwise) to tighten and to the right (clockwise) to loosen. If the rim is raised, tighten the spokes (left and right equally) along the affected part of the rim. If it is flattened, loosen the spokes similarly.

The tyre treads should be regularly checked for the slightest cut in which foreign bodies might get lodged. Any such foreign bodies should be removed carefully using a sharp object with the tyre deflated. If you ride over loose chippings, broken glass or the like, you should hold a gloved hand against each wheel while still riding so as to remove any sharp stones or pieces of glass before they get embedded in the treads. This should hopefully prevent a puncture occurring.

Sticking on tubulars with rim cement
If the rim is a new one, you must first clean it carefully with petrol to remove any oil, grease or metal dust. You should then apply rim cement in three or four layers so as to build up a good bed. Each layer should be thin but evenly distributed. The first layer should be given 24 hours to dry, the other layers ten hours apiece.

A new tyre is usually difficult to get onto the rim, and must first be carefully stretched. This can be done by stepping on the tyre and pulling it up with both hands, then doing the same all the way round. You can now apply the last layer of rim cement. Let it dry for five or ten minutes, then start to pull the tyre on over the rim. Partially inflate the tyre, and begin with the valve at the top, working down either side around the rim with both hands. To finish the job, place the wheel horizontally (over your thigh, for example), and push the remaining part of the tyre onto the rim with your thumb.

Once you have fitted the tyre, you should rotate the wheel to check that the tyre is lying correctly on the rim. If it needs straightening at any point, push or pull the offending section with your thumb and the palm of your hand until it lies centrally over the rim. Finally pump the tyre up to five or six atmospheres, and leave it to dry for half a day before using the wheel on a ride.

If the rim has been used before, it will already have a bed of cement. Sometimes the bed is still sticky enough to fit the tyre without any additional rim cement. This means that a spare tyre can be quickly fitted after a puncture during training or competition – though the tyre must have been used so that it is well stretched and has some rim cement still left on it.

Sticking on tubulars with rim tape
If you prefer double-sided rim tape to cement, you should again start by cleaning the rim. When sticking the tape on, start at the valve hole and work your way round, pressing the tape flat with a blunt object such as a screwdriver handle.

Now moisten the whole length of the tape with water so as to avoid the tyre sticking fast before it has been properly straightened. Then pull on the tyre in the same way as with rim cement. With rim tape you can ride the bike as soon as the tyre has been fitted.

Indoor training aids

The weather is often unsuitable for outdoor cycling, and this means that indoor cycle training forms an essential part of a triathlete's training programme. There are two contraptions that make such training possible: training rollers and the home trainer. Both have their advantages and disadvantages.

Training rollers have the advantage that you can ride your own familiar bike on them. However, they only provide effective training if there is sufficient resistance to ride against. This is only possible on machines that have at least one roller at the front and two at the back. Front and back rollers must be linked together by means of a V-belt.

Some training rollers have an extra attachment that imitates the effect of wind resistance. This provides yet another training load to work against.

The **home trainer** is a more sophisticated device for simulating the conditions of a training ride. Thanks to advances in computer technology, the latest home trainers are getting closer and closer to actual training conditions. Some machines can even create the effect of a climb by means of a special brake mechanism.

Clothing for training

The one-piece triathlon suit is worn for all three parts of a triathlon contest (see page 17). But there are certain items that are specific to the cycling part of the event. These should be chosen in order to:

- ensure the maximum transfer of power (shoes)
- make the rider as comfortable as possible (shorts and mitts)
- give maximum protection against the weather (jersey and weatherproofs)
- provide adequate protection in accidents (crash hat).

The following items of clothing are absolutely essential for cycle training:

Cycle-racing shoes
These should be fitted with velcro fastenings so as to save time during the change-over between disciplines.

Cycling shorts
The leather insert must be kept soft and supple by rubbing in vaseline before training, and it should not be allowed to form creases.

Cycling jersey
The jersey should be more than long

This home trainer can be used with your competition bike.

enough to cover up the lumbar region while riding. The kidneys must be properly protected against the cold. Loud, bright colours are a good safety precaution, making you readily visible in traffic.

Weatherproofs
You need one of the newly developed materials that is not only weatherproof but also "breathes". Rain and wind must be prevented from getting in, but sweat and condensation must be able to get out.

Cycle-racing shoes with velcro fastenings.

A suitable crash hat.

Crash hat

A good crash hat should be light but sufficiently sturdy to protect the head from injury in a crash. The aerodynamic shape of a time-trial hat is of particular interest to triathletes.

Track mitts

These not only prevent scratching or grazing in a crash, but also stop blisters from developing during long rides. They can also be used to remove foreign bodies from the tyres while still riding (see page 32).

Running

Running shoes

The shoes are undoubtedly the most important item of equipment, and no expense should be spared in order to make sure they are right. Running makes heavy demands on the bones, joints and ligaments in the legs and feet. A 10 km run entails an average of 6,500 steps, and each step exerts a force equivalent to about two or three times the weight of the runner. For a runner weighing 75 kg (165 pounds or 12 stone), this comes to 150–220 kg (335–490 pounds or 24–35 stone)! The impact is transferred via the foot to the joints in the ankle, knee and hip. So it is vitally important to match the shoes to the individual runner so that they help to minimise, if not totally prevent, any injuries in the joints that are affected.

The biomechanical analysis of running movements, combined with the development of new materials, has lead to a continual improvement in the choice and quality of running shoes available. But is a different matter knowing which model is the right one for you. Do you need a curved last or a straight last? – a special heel wedge or none at all? – a heavy shoe or a light shoe? – a studded tread or a completely smooth tread?

General requirements for a good shoe

- A three-part sole made up of:
  a tread studded for safety in all ground conditions;
  a midsole made of soft porous rubber for shock absorption;
  a heel wedge.
- A strong heel counter so that the foot is held firmly in the shoe.
- A soft Achilles tab so as to avoid pressure on the Achilles tendon.
- An upper made of light material (usually layered nylon, but occasionally leather) that fits well without constricting the foot.
- Plenty of room for the toes.
- Heavier shoes providing greater stability for training, with lighter shoes for competitions.

Special individual requirements

The two commonest foot problems that require special attention are raised arches and fallen arches or flat feet. Fallen arches are characterised by flat soles and a tendency to bend the feet inwards (pronation). If you are one of the

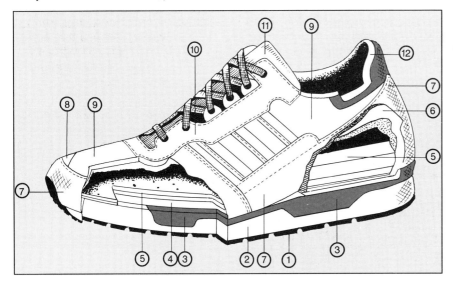

Typical features of a good running shoe:
1 Flexible rubber tread.
2 Midsole base made of soft, shock-absorbent polyurethane.
3 Midsole upper made of a harder polyurethane and raised at the back to protect the heel.
4 Flexible full moccasin construction.
5 Insole well moulded to the foot and efficient at soaking away sweat.
6 Long heel counter to support and guide the foot.
7 Velour trim all the way round.
8 Sewn-in toecap.
9 Shoe upper made of light nylon mesh that allows the foot to breathe.
10 Lace arrangement easy to tighten and adjust.
11 Well-padded tongue.
12 Soft, well-padded Achilles tab.

Special adaptations for running shoes

Foot position while running	Cause	Special adaptation required
pronation (foot bent inwards, putting pressure on the inside edge)	fallen arch	a special heel wedge, hard towards the inside edge and soft towards the outside edge a firm heel counter, pulled forwards along the inside of the foot a heel stabiliser – a special strap inserted between the sole and the heel counter
	knock knees	as above, plus a firm shoe with a straight last
supination (foot bent outwards, putting pressure on the outside edge)	raised arch	well cushioned under the ball of the foot plenty of room in the toe area
	bow legs	a special midsole insert at the front, hard towards the outside edge and soft towards the inside ege an upper made of firm material at the front
foot straight		a symmetrically built shoe without any special inserts in the midsole

many people with flat feet, you will need special corrective inserts under the heel. Otherwise it will only be a matter of time before you get pains in the leg joints, especially around the outside of the knees.

If you have raised arches you will have a tendency to bend your feet outwards (supination). Make sure you have thick shock-absorbent padding under the ball of the foot, and plenty of room for the toes, with a space of 3–4 mm between the tips of the toes and the end of the shoe.

Such precautions do not apply only to top performers. Indeed, all runners should make sure that their shoes are carefully matched to their own feet. To do this accurately usually requires orthopaedic inserts made of a special material. Orthopaedic specialists use a treadmill and a video camera in order to analyse individual foot movements and correct the shoe accordingly. Sometimes a change of shoes is enough to correct minor problems. For this reason it is also important to have at least two pairs of shoes for use over different kinds of terrain, with soft soles for running on roads and harder soles for soft ground.

Clothing for training

The ideal material for training clothes is one which has the ability to soak up

sweat from the skin and transfer it to the outside where it can evaporate. In cold weather the skin should be kept dry and warm, whereas in hot weather the heat must be allowed to escape. If the best performance is to be achieved, clothing should not be too heavy, and should fit snugly without constricting movement.

Legwear
Running shorts and tracksuit bottoms are needed for use in warm and cold weather respectively. Long johns under tracksuit bottoms provide further insulation in really cold weather.

Shirts
A variety of clothes is needed to cater for different kinds of weather: T-shirts, long-sleeved skiing vests made of quick-drying materials, sweatshirts and sleeveless string vests.

Socks
These should fit snugly, and should be made of a good absorbent material; cotton is the best.

Analysing foot movements using a treadmill and a video camera.

Technique

In all sports the relationship between ability and performance is a very complex one, and depends on a variety of factors. Apart from tactical ability and the various external and psychological factors, there are five main elements that affect performance: technique, flexibility, strength, speed and endurance.

Technique can be defined as the coordination of the muscles and central nervous system in order to produce a specific set of movements. Technique, or coordination, is basically the creation of movement. Good technique is characterised by the economic use of movement, in which the minimum of energy is used to maximum effect.

Endurance sports involve the frequent repetition of movements, which means that technique is a particularly important factor in determining performance. The more efficient the technique, the less energy is used to produce the same level of performance, and the longer that performance can be sustained using the same amount of energy. Thus technique also plays a vital role in reducing fatigue.

Technical training

Technical training for the triathlon involves specific training in all three disciplines of swimming, cycling and running. It should as far as possible be geared towards the physical make-up of each individual triathlete.

Good technical training brings about advantages in other areas too. Learning capacity is enhanced, enabling further technical improvement. The athlete also learns to adapt to changing circumstances such as swimming through waves, cycling against the wind or running over rough terrain. Technical exercises also help to bring variety into the training programme.

Frequent and concentrated repetition of technical exercises makes heavy demands on the central nervous system, which according to recent scientific

research is one of the first parts of the body to suffer from fatigue – before such areas as the heart, circulation and metabolic systems. The training programme should therefore be planned so that technical training always comes before conditioning training (general aerobic and anaerobic endurance, strength endurance), and preferably when the athlete is well rested.

High-performance training usually involves two or three training sessions a day. So technical training should be incorporated in the programme next to the recovery periods that follow the various training efforts. Here is an example of how this might work in practice:

■ The triathlete is well rested for the first training session. Exercises in coordination and technique are at their most effective at this stage.

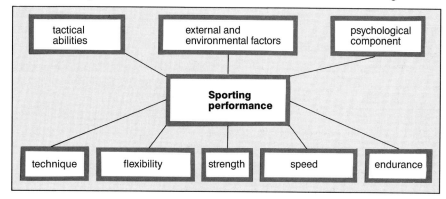

Elements of sporting performance.

The basic elements of performance and their importance in the triathlon

Elements	Definitions	Training methods	Effects of training	Relevance to the triathlon
technique (coordination)	coordination of the muscles and central nervous system within a specific set of movements	practising movements; specific technical exercises	greater economy of movement; less expenditure of energy and less fatigue following the same level of performance	• swimming, cycling and running technique • changes of clothing, movement and rhythm
mobility (flexibility)	the amount of deliberate movement that is possible in the joints	stretching and loosening exercises	stretching of the musclature	in swimming especially, a good technique is only possible when there is sufficient mobility; a stretched muscle is also more powerful
strength	the ability of a muscle to produce a certain tension in order to: • move the body or an item of equipment (dynamic strength) • work against a resistance (static strength) • overcome a resistance in the shortest possible time (muscular power)	various strength training methods, depending on the requirements of the particular sport: • maximum strength • musclar power • muscular endurance • isokinetic training	changes in muscles, bones, tendons and ligaments; increased strength due to increased muscle size	in swimming especially, a good technique is only possible when there is sufficient mobility; a stretched muscle is also more powerful
speed (agility)	the ability to react quickly to a stimulus and to carry out movements at high speed	shortening the reaction time so as to perform each movement faster and more often, thus increasing the overall speed	improvements in technique and musculature	the swimming start, change-overs and tactical manoeuvres such as overtaking
endurance (stamina)	the ability to sustain a given performance level over the longest possible period general aerobic endurance general anaerobic endurance (speed endurance, staying power)	low- to medium-intensity loading of the main muscle groups over a set period of time high-intensity loading of the main muscle groups over a shorter period	improvements in the musculature and in the efficiency of the heart and cardiovascular system improved muscle metabolism in order to sustain a good performance under oxygen debt with high blood lactate levels	the most important factor determining performance in all three disciplines and in the triathlon as a whole

- Technical training can be repeated at the beginning of the second training session, with just two provisos. Firstly, there should be a recovery period of at least two to three hours between the first and second sessions. Secondly, the conditioning training in the first section should not have been at too high an intensity.
- The third session should not include any specific technical exercises, as the central nervous system in particular will already have become fatigued as a result of the two preceding training sessions.

Swimming

In order to develop a high level of technical competence, you must first make a detailed study of all the movements involved. This is only possible if you are familiar with the laws of physics as they affect swimming, and take due note of them in practice.

The physics of swimming

Buoyancy

This is the upward force exerted by the water on a body that is immersed in it. It works according to Archimedes' Principle, which states that the upward force exerted on a body in liquid is the same as the weight of the volume of liquid that it displaces. So if a person's body is of the same weight as that of the volume of water displaced, then that person will float in the water.

The point upon which the buoyancy of a body appears to act is called the *centre of buoyancy* (CB). Buoyancy works in the opposite direction to gravity, which appears to act upon the *centre of gravity* (CG). The shorter the distance between

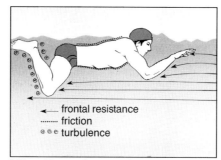

frontal resistance
friction
turbulence

Different types of water resistance.

these two points, the better a swimmer's position in the water – though the situation varies from swimmer to swimmer.

Water resistance

This is the force acting against the swimmer as he moves through the water. There are three types of water resistance involved: frontal resistance, friction and turbulence. As the swimming speed increases, the water resistance increases according to the square of the speed.

The flatter a swimmer's position in the water, the less water resistance occurs. Water resistance is also increased by any arm and leg movements that run counter to the swimming direction. These should therefore be carried out as slowly as possible.

Propulsion

This is the force that carries the swimmer forward. According to Newton's Third Law

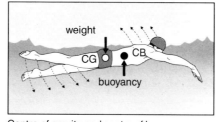

Centre of gravity and centre of buoyancy.

of Motion, to every action there is an equal and opposite reaction. When you are running, for example, your feet push backwards and downwards on the ground and your body reacts by moving forwards and upwards. The same principle of action and reaction can be applied to swimming. The arms and hands must push backwards in order to push the body forwards through the water.

There is, however, a limiting factor in that water is not solid, so that the pressure exerted on it will also set the water in motion. The arms and hands should therefore move in such a way as to keep the water movement to the minimum possible given the pressure required to propel the body forward. The ideal configuration is zigzag or double-S formation, just like a ship's propeller. The fingers should also be slightly spread in order to produce the maximum propulsion.

There are a number of other laws of fluid mechanics that are important to swimming propulsion – Bernoulli's Principle, for example. Details of these can be found in specialist books on swimming.

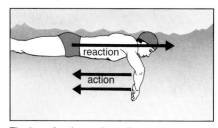

The law of action and reaction.

Generally speaking, however, propulsion must be uniform in order to be most economic and effective. This means that all strokes should be carried out evenly without any changes of rhythm.

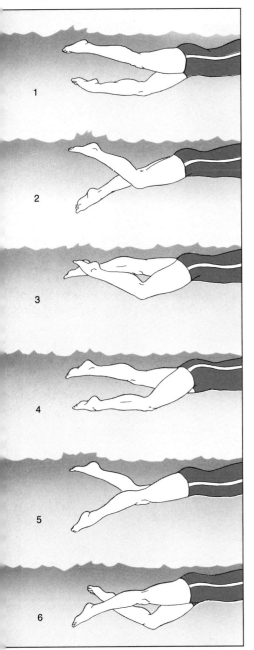

The legstroke in the crawl.

The crawl stroke

Legstroke

The legs play only a secondary role in propulsion, their chief task being to keep the body stable in the water. The alternate armstrokes create sideways movements that hinder progress, and these need to be balanced. The legs should be used to keep the body in the ideal position where the water resistance is least.

The stroke is initiated from the hip (1). As the thigh pushes downwards, the water resistance causes the knee to bend involuntarily (2). The leg is deliberately straightened with a kick, creating a certain amount of propulsion (3, 4). The leg is raised again, almost involuntarily, as a counter-movement to the other legstroke (5, 6).

Armstroke

The alternating armstroke provides most of the propulsion in the crawl. It is made up of three phases: the pull and push (underwater) phases and the swing or recovery phrase.

The pull phase begins as the hand takes hold of the water, with the arm turned slightly inwards (1, 2). The hand is turned outwards while the elbow is gradually bent, and the upper arm, lower arm and hand are pulled backwards, propelling the body forwards (3).

As the arm reaches shoulder level, the elbow reaches its maximum angle of 90° and the push phase begins (4, 5). This ends with the arm nearly straight so that the thumb is almost touching the thigh. In the recovery phase the elbow is raised out of the water (6) and then the arm swings forwards without the muscles being tensed very much.

Rolling the body in the water gives assistance to the armstroke by creating body angles that help to coordinate the muscles responsible for propulsion. If the shoulder joint is lacking in flexibility, rolling the body helps at the beginning of the recovery phase by ensuring that the arm is brought forward in a straight line.

Coordination

The armstrokes and legstrokes usually work together naturally without conscious effort. The ideal combination depends on the individual triathlete, his position in the water and the length of the course; it may vary from two to six legstrokes for each pair of armstrokes (one right, one left). The longer the swimming distance, the fewer the legstrokes that should be used. Most triathletes save energy by using the two-stroke combination, in which the armstrokes and legstrokes reinforce each other: the triathlete immerses his right arm at the same time as he kicks with his left leg, and vice versa.

Breathing

This should be incorporated into the swimming strokes so as not to disturb either the alternating rhythm of the armstrokes or the position of the body in the water, say by raising the head to breathe. The swimmer breathes out underwater through the nose and mouth. Then when the "breathing arm" is raised out of the water, the rolling motion helps to bring the mouth out of the water too, so that the swimmer can breathe in the trough behind the bow wave.

Triathletes vary in the breathing rhythms that they use. Breathing in once every two armstrokes often creates a certain lopsidedness; the arms pull with different strengths, and it is difficult to navigate when you can only see on one side of your body. Breathing once every three strokes makes it easier to swim straight in open water, but makes heavier demands on breathing capacity (the swimmer breathes out during the second

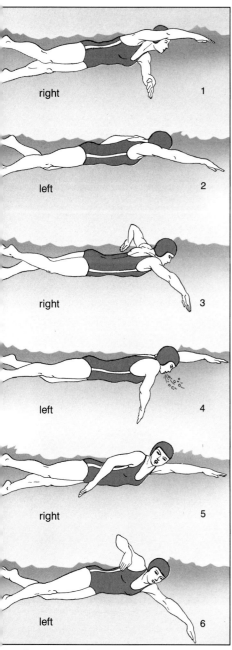

right 1

left 2

right 3

left 4

right 5

left 6

complete crawl stroke.

The armstroke in the crawl.

1

2

3

4

5

6

take hold of the water

bend the elbow

push the water away

raise the elbow

and third armstrokes). One compromise is to alternate between two-stroke and three-stroke breathing.

Learning exercises

The following exercises are intended for improving the basic crawl stroke. They should first be practised in a swimming pool with the body well rested (immediately after warm-up). Experience suggests that a good crawl technique cannot be achieved all at once. So you should first concentrate on the arms and legs separately, and only then go on to look at the whole stroke, finally adding the breathing.

Improving the legstroke

- Sit on the edge of the pool with your legs in the water, and move your legs to and fro in alternation, taking care to emphasise the kicking movement.
- Practise the legstroke on your front with your arms straight, holding on to the edge of the pool.
- Practise the legstroke on your back with your head supported by a float.

- Practise the legstroke on your front with flippers and a float, keeping your head in the water.
- Practise the legstroke on your front using a float with your arms straight.
- Practise the legstroke on your front without using a float.

Likely faults	Ways of correcting them
■ "Cycling"—pulling your knees up under your stomach, and failing to initiate from the hip.	• Move your legs out straighter. • Practise the legstroke on your back, holding a float across your stomach between your hips.
■ Turning your toes back so that there is no surface area for propulsion.	• Stretch your toes, turning them slightly inwards. • Practise the legstroke on your front using flippers.
■ Legstrokes too small, resulting in a hurried, uncoordinated technique.	• Practise slowly and gently, consciously widening the legstroke until you find the most effective technique.

More exercises for improving the legstroke

- Practise the legstroke on your front, holding your hands over your back.
- Practise the legstroke on your side, holding the lower arm out in front of you and the upper arm to your side (see drawing).
- Practise the legstroke underwater.
- Contrast exercise: swim 10 m of legstroke with your knees drawn up under your stomach ("cycling"), then return to the correct stroke.

- Contrast exercise: swim 10 m of legstroke with your toes turned back, then return to the correct stroke.

Improving the armstroke

- Go to where the water reaches your hips and practise the armstroke with your feet walking along the bottom, starting with your head above water and then underwater.
- Partner exercise: partner 1 holds partner 2 by the feet and pushes him through the water, while partner 2 practises the armstroke with his face underwater.
- Practise the armstroke using a float or a pullbuoy, and without breathing.

Likely faults

- In the recovery phase your arms swing too far sideways. Your body reacts by swinging to the opposite side to compensate.

Ways of correcting them

- Raise your elbow up high, turning the back of your hand outwards, and exaggerating the rolling motion of your body.
- Raise your elbow so high that your thumb is drawn up the side of your body as far as your armpit.

- Practise the armstroke while swimming along close to the side of the pool, taking care to raise your elbow up high.

More exercises for improving the armstroke

- Practise with one arm only, with the other arm held out straight supported by a float.
- Practise with one arm only, but without using a float.
- Place your thumbs in your armpits and practise the alternating armstroke "chicken-style" with your arms thus shortened. Use a vigorous legstroke, with or without flippers.
- Practise the armstroke using swim paddles, with or without a pullbuoy.
- Contrast exercise: swim 10 m of armstroke with your arms straight both underwater and above, then return to the correct stroke with your elbows bent.
- Contrast exercise: swim 10 m of armstroke with fists clenched or fingers splayed, then return to the normal hand formation.

- Your arms swing too far across the front of your body.

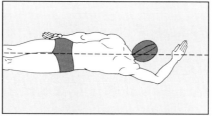

- During the underwater phase your arms are too straight or too close to the mid-line of your body.

- Your hands and arms are pulling downwards instead of backwards, pushing up the front of your body.

- Your elbow sinks down during the pull phase.

- Place your arm well forward in the water, out in front of your shoulder.

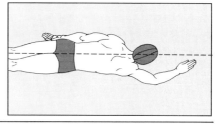

- Try to touch your stomach with your thumb.
- Practise the stroke out of the water in front of the mirror or using a pulley rope.

- Keep your elbows up during the underwater phase too; the push phase doesn't finish until your thumb is almost touching your thigh.

- Practise out of the water as above.
- Keep your elbows up underwater as previously.

The complete stroke without the breathing

- Push off from the side and practise the complete crawl stroke without breathing, standing on the bottom to breathe.
- Practise one-armed crawl using a float. Breathe at first by standing on the bottom, then by raising your head without interrupting the flow, and finally by turning your head.
- Practise one-armed crawl without a float, exaggerating the rolling motion.

Likely faults

- The legstroke is weak or perhaps even non-existent.

- For other faults and ways of correcting them, see legstroke and armstroke on pages 42 and 43.

Ways of correcting them

- Start with the legstroke only, and only bring the arms in later.

Improving the breathing

- Go to where the water reaches your hips and practise the armstroke on one side with the other hand holding the overflow channel. Breathe out during the whole of the underwater phase, and breathe in when your elbow comes out of the water.
- Go to where the water reaches your hips, bend over and practise armstroke and breathing together, with your legs walking along the bottom.
- Practise legstroke and breathing together. Consciously breathe out into the water and breathe in by turning your head.
- Partner exercise as for armstroke, but this time practise armstroke and breathing together.

Likely faults

- Your head comes up to breathe.

Ways of correcting them

- Concentrate on rolling your body; when you breathe in, look at the side of the pool and keep your head floating in the water.

The complete stroke together with the breathing

- Pushing off from the side, practise the complete crawl stroke including the breathing; swim for 10–15 m, then start again.
- Practise the whole stroke, exaggerating the rolling motion of your body.
- Practise with one arm and both legs.
- Practise the crawl, breathing on the side you are not used to.

Likely faults

- Your armstroke is uneven or you are out of breath after only a few strokes. First you hold your breath, then the push phase is over before you have finished breathing out, and you have too little time out of the water to breathe out and in.

- For other faults and ways of correcting them, see all previous sections on legstroke, armstroke, breathing and the complete stroke without breathing.

Ways of correcting them

- Breathe out consciously into the water.
- Start breathing out when the "breathing arm" enters the pull phase.
- Practise breathing out against the water resistance.

- Catch-up swimming: the first arm out front waits for the other arm to catch up before starting the underwater phase; the legstroke must be stronger to compensate.
- Practise the crawl stroke with both legs kicking simultaneously.

More exercises for improving the complete stroke together with the breathing

- Coordination exercise: varying the legstroke rhythm, first two strokes and then six strokes for each pair of armstrokes.
- Breathing exercise: start breathing once every two strokes, then once every three, four and five strokes etc, until you have swum a whole length.
- Contrast exercise: swim 10 m of crawl, keeping the armstrokes short, fast and unfinished; then return to long armstrokes reaching back to the thigh.
- Run through a whole series of varied techniques within a single length. You might start, for example, with legstrokes on your front, side and back, followed by two left armstrokes, two right armstrokes and four alternating armstrokes.

Area of frontal resistance in relation to body position.

Cycling

The physics of cycling

There are three types of resistance which a cyclist must overcome: rolling resistance, wind resistance and resistance due to gravity. Rolling resistance has already been explained in the section on tyres (see page 26).

Wind resistance (F_W)

This is the resistance of the air that the cyclist is riding into. The amount of wind resistance can be worked out using the following formula:

$$F_W = A \times c_w \times \frac{\varrho}{2} \times v^2$$

A = the frontal area (in square metres) presented by the rider and his machine.

c_w = the wind resistance coefficient, which is affected by the texture of the rider's clothing and by the aerodynamics of his posture and of the bicycle itself.

ϱ = the density of the atmosphere, which is 1.23 kg/m³ on flat land at sea level, but which decreases with increasing height.

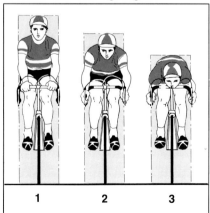

1   2   3

v^2 = the square of the velocity of the air meeting the rider, consisting of the wind velocity plus the velocity of the bike.

The wind resistance increases according to the square of the speed. So the higher the performance level, the more important it is to reduce the wind resistance to a minimum. The formula above has the following practical implications:

- The area of frontal resistance should be as small as possible. It is noticeably reduced if the hands are on the drops instead of on the tops of the bars.

Area of frontal resistance.

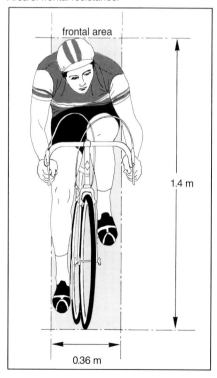

frontal area

1.4 m

0.36 m

Body position and hand position.

■ The wind resistance coefficient should not be increased unnecessarily. Skin-tight clothing is therefore desirable. Aerodynamic bicycle components are a considerable advantage at the high-performance level. It is also important to adopt a low, well-streamlined posture.

Resistance due to gravity (F_G)
This occurs when cycling uphill, meaning that extra effort is required when riding in hilly terrain.

$$F_G = F_N \times \frac{h}{l}$$

F_N = the force equivalent to the weight of the rider and machine.
h = the height difference of the slope.
l = the length of the slope.

A rider who weighs less is at an advantage when cycling uphill, but will be slower coming downhill than a heavier rider. As the speed is less when cycling uphill, the wind resistance is much lower and an aerodynamic posture is not so important.

Riding posture

Riding posture depends largely on the position of the hands on the bars (see drawings above). Cyclists distinguish between three different hand positions:

On the tops
The hands hold the tops of the bars at the same distance either side of the stem. The body is relatively upright, and this helps take the weight off the back, which is otherwise bent over. One disadvantage is that the rider has less control over the bike than in the other riding positions. But this position is especially suitable for training rides, for long, gentle climbs, or simply to relieve the back muscles.

On the hoods
This is an intermediate position in which the hands hold the brake-lever hoods between the thumb and forefinger. This grip is used by many riders on steeper climbs (see Climbing position, page 49), which place heavy demands on the arm and back muscles. The brake levers are within easy reach. Riding on the hoods is also good for longer training rides, as it combines a comfortable posture with relatively low wind resistance.

On the drops
The hands grip the dropped part of the bars below the brake levers. This creates an aerodynamic posture with low wind resistance, making it most suitable for cycling downhill, against the wind, or when racing on the level. The body is

bent right over, but the rider has very good control and the brakes are within easy reach.

Round pedalling

Cycling performance depends primarily on the action of the legs. You must do the following to ensure optimum energy transmission:

■ Try actively to propel the bike forwards at every stage of the pedal revolution.
■ Apply the affected muscle groups in a continuous, uninterrupted flow.
■ Always try to push or pull at right angles to the crank throughout the pedal revolution (see diagram on page 48).
■ Adjust the pedalling action so that the same amount of force is applied at every point in the revolution.

The pedalling action must be round and even, or else unnecessary power and energy will be lost. You cannot begin to create a round pedalling action unless shoe and pedal are firmly locked together, either with a toeclip and strap or with a safety pedal.

When describing pedalling, it is normal to divide the revolution into four sectors (see diagram opposite). In the top sector there is a critical point to be overcome ("top dead centre"), where a pulling force gives way to a pushing force; the foot pushes forwards (1). In the next sector the energy transmission is at its best and the foot presses downwards (2). In the lower sector is the second critical point ("bottom dead centre"), where the leg stops straightening in the pushing phase and starts to bend in the the pulling phase; the toe points downwards (3). In the last sector the energy transmission is worst; the foot is pulled upwards (4).

There are few specific exercises for improving pedalling style. Round pedalling can only be achieved by plenty of long rides using low gears at high pedalling rates. One way is to use a fixed wheel – a hub without a freewheel. This compels the rider to pedal constantly and helps to develop a round pedalling style. You should mount a single sprocket with perhaps 17 or 18 teeth, and shorten the chain to the correct length. You should first try out a fixed wheel on a quiet stretch of road, so that you can learn how to reduce speed and brake correctly.

Another useful exercise is one-legged riding, which allows you to concentrate on the pulling phase of the pedal revolution. Choose a flat course of up to 1,000 m and use medium gearing.

It is vital throughout to achieve good coordination between the two legs, which should always be moving parallel to the frame.

Round pedalling.

The best pedalling rate

The results of laboratory tests suggest that the most economic pedalling rate is between 40 and 60 revolutions per minute (rpm). But the analysis of world-record performances over the last 40 years gives a very much higher rate of around 100–110 rpm. Even higher rates have been achieved on training runs. High pedalling rates over long periods are the only way of developing a good, efficient pedalling style. In the triathlon especially, the pedalling rate should only ever be low on climbs.

The gearing

A number of different gear combinations must be available in order to achieve the best pedalling rate in a variety of different situations. You must take account of:

- the individual performance capacity (level of training).
- the course profile (climbs and descents).
- wind conditions (head wind or tail wind).
- road conditions.

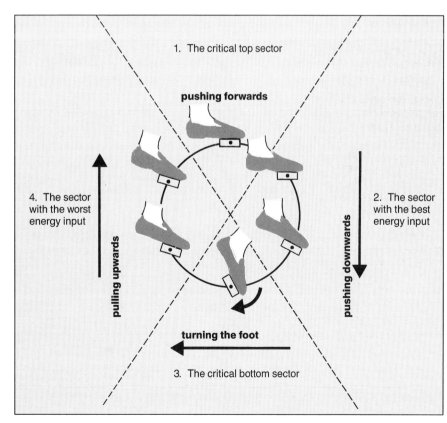

1. The critical top sector

pushing forwards

4. The sector with the worst energy input

2. The sector with the best energy input

pulling upwards

pushing downwards

turning the foot

3. The critical bottom sector

48

The gear ratio can be worked out from the number of teeth on the chainwheel and freewheel sprockets respectively. The value obtained indicates the number of turns made by the freewheel (and hence the back wheel) for every pedal revolution. If the result is multiplied by the diameter of the back wheel (27″ on racing bikes), this gives the gear ratio in inches (R_I).

$$R_I = \frac{n_1}{n_2} \times 27$$

n_1 = the number of teeth on the chainwheel.

n_2 = the number of teeth on the sprocket.

In order to work out how many metres the wheel travels for each pedal revolution, the gear ratio in inches is converted into metres (1″ = 0.0254 m) and the result is multiplied by π (3.14), giving the gear ratio in metres (R_M).

$$R_M = R_I \times 0.0254 \times \pi$$
$$= \frac{n_1}{n_2} \times 27 \times 0.0254 \times 3.14$$
$$= \frac{n_1}{n_2} \times 2.15$$

Triathletes normally use two chainwheels and six or seven freewheel sprockets, giving a theoretical maximum of 12 or 14 gears. But friction in the chain (see page 24) prevents the larger chainwheel from being used with the smallest sprocket, or the smaller chainwheel with the largest sprocket.

Gear ratios are compiled in the form of gear tables (see opposite). Using these makes it much easier to select a suitable range of gears and to avoid choosing two combinations that produce nearly the same gear ratio. Note the following when deciding between two such combinations:

- It is better to use the combination with the largest number of teeth altogether, because this makes the pedalling action smoother.
- It is better to use the combination that brings the chain closest to the ideal chainline (see page 25), so that chain friction is reduced to a minimum.

Other factors must also be taken into consideration. The resulting gear changes must be such that rhythmic pedalling can continue at a medium or high rate in spite of any changes of terrain or conditions.

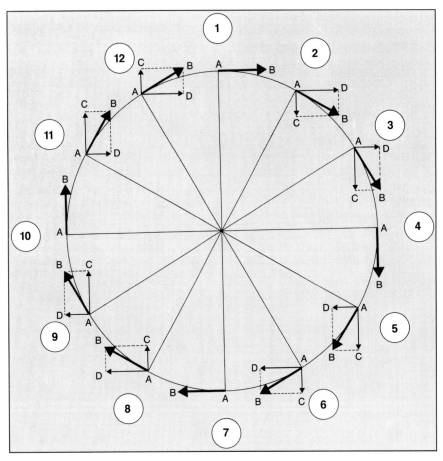

The ideal distribution of pedalling forces. At all stages of the pedal revolution, the horizontal (A–D) and vertical (A–C) forces should be such as to create the maximum resulting force (A–B) working at right angles to the crank. The size of the forces is shown by the lengths of the arrows in the diagram. The force of leverage should ideally work at right angles to the crank.

High gear ratios of more than 90″ require an enormous power input to sustain even a low pedalling rate. In the triathlon they are only used by high-performance triathletes and/or on downhill stretches. Ratios of around 90″ (52:15 or 52:16) can, however, be used even for long periods in competitions at a fairly economical pedalling rate. Medium ratios of 70–90″ are more suitable for training or for medium or long triathlons.

With low gear ratios (less than 70″) the pedalling rate is high but the power input is low. They are used in basic training in order to develop a fast pedalling rate and a round, efficient pedalling style. During the competition period they can be used for regenerative training periods involving active recuperation.

Climbing position

The climbing position is used mainly for short, steep climbs and for fast acceleration after sharp corners or when setting off. The body weight should be used to full advantage. It should always be over the straight leg, while the bike is pulled over towards the opposite side.

The hands should be positioned on the hoods, enabling the arm, torso and back muscles to be fully engaged. The centre of gravity should not be too far forward, as this can allow the back wheel to slip. On the other hand, if the centre of gravity is too far back, this will prevent the effective use of the arm and torso muscles. Expert climbers alternate regularly between a sitting and a standing position, known as "honking".

The climbing position can, indeed should, be practised on the level, using gears that require a great deal of pedalling effort from the sitting position.

Gear table in inches

Sprocket	Chainwheel														
No. of teeth	42	43	44	45	46	47	48	49	50	51	52	53	54	55	56
12	94.5	96.8	99.0	101.3	103.5	105.8	108.0	110.3	112.5	114.8	117.0	119.3	121.5	123.8	126.0
13	87.2	89.3	91.4	93.4	95.4	97.5	99.8	101.8	103.8	105.8	108.1	110.0	112.1	114.2	116.3
14	81.0	82.9	84.9	86.8	88.7	90.6	92.5	94.5	96.4	98.4	100.3	102.2	104.2	106.0	107.8
15	75.6	77.4	79.2	81.0	82.8	84.6	86.4	88.2	90.0	91.8	93.6	95.4	97.2	99.0	100.8
16	70.9	72.5	74.3	76.0	77.6	79.3	81.0	82.7	84.4	86.1	87.8	89.5	91.2	92.8	94.5
17	66.7	68.3	69.9	71.5	73.0	74.6	76.2	77.8	79.4	81.0	82.6	84.2	85.6	87.3	88.9
18	63.0	64.5	66.0	67.5	69.0	70.5	72.0	73.5	75.0	76.5	78.0	79.5	81.0	82.5	84.0
19	59.7	61.1	62.5	64.0	65.4	66.8	68.2	69.6	71.1	72.5	73.9	75.4	76.7	78.0	79.4
20	56.7	58.1	59.4	60.8	62.1	63.5	64.8	66.2	67.5	68.9	70.2	71.6	72.8	74.2	75.6
21	54.0	55.3	56.6	57.9	59.1	60.4	61.7	63.0	64.3	65.6	66.9	68.1	69.4	70.7	72.0
22	51.5	52.8	54.0	55.2	56.5	57.7	58.9	60.1	61.4	62.6	63.8	65.0	66.3	67.5	68.7
23	49.3	50.5	51.7	52.8	54.0	55.2	56.3	57.5	58.7	59.9	61.0	62.2	63.3	64.5	65.7
24	47.3	48.4	49.5	50.6	51.8	52.9	54.0	55.1	56.3	57.4	58.5	59.6	60.7	61.8	63.0
25	45.4	46.4	47.5	48.6	49.7	50.8	51.8	52.9	54.0	55.1	56.2	57.4	58.3	59.4	60.4
26	43.6	44.6	45.7	46.7	47.8	48.8	49.8	50.9	51.9	52.9	54.0	55.0	56.1	57.1	58.1

Gear table in metres

Sprocket	Chainwheel														
No. of teeth	42	43	44	45	46	47	48	49	50	51	52	53	54	55	56
12	7.47	7.65	7.83	8.01	8.18	8.36	8.54	8.72	8.90	9.07	9.25	9.43	9.61	9.79	9.97
13	6.90	7.06	7.23	7.39	7.55	7.72	7.88	8.05	8.21	8.38	8.54	8.70	8.87	9.03	9.20
14	6.40	6.56	6.71	6.86	7.01	7.17	7.32	7.47	7.63	7.78	7.93	8.08	8.23	8.39	8.54
15	5.98	6.12	6.26	6.40	6.55	6.69	6.83	6.97	7.12	7.26	7.40	7.54	7.69	7.83	7.97
16	5.60	5.74	5.87	6.00	6.14	6.27	6.40	6.54	6.67	6.81	6.94	7.07	7.20	7.34	7.47
17	5.27	5.40	5.52	5.65	5.78	5.90	6.03	6.15	6.28	6.40	6.53	6.66	6.78	6.91	7.03
18	4.98	5.10	5.22	5.34	5.45	5.57	5.69	5.81	5.93	6.05	6.17	6.29	6.40	6.52	6.64
19	4.72	4.83	4.94	5.05	5.17	5.28	5.39	5.50	5.62	5.73	5.84	5.95	6.07	6.18	6.29
20	4.48	4.59	4.70	4.80	4.91	5.02	5.12	5.23	5.34	5.44	5.55	5.66	5.76	5.87	5.98
21	4.27	4.37	4.47	4.57	4.67	4.78	4.88	4.98	5.08	5.18	5.29	5.39	5.49	5.59	5.69
22	4.07	4.17	4.27	4.37	4.46	4.56	4.66	4.75	4.85	4.95	5.04	5.14	5.24	5.34	5.43
23	3.90	3.99	4.08	4.18	4.27	4.36	4.45	4.55	4.64	4.73	4.83	4.92	5.01	5.10	5.20
24	3.73	3.82	3.91	4.00	4.09	4.18	4.27	4.36	4.45	4.54	4.62	4.71	4.80	4.89	4.98
25	3.58	3.67	3.76	3.84	3.93	4.01	4.10	4.18	4.27	4.35	4.44	4.52	4.61	4.69	4.78
26	3.45	3.53	3.61	3.69	3.78	3.86	3.94	4.02	4.10	4.19	4.27	4.35	4.43	4.51	4.60

Cornering

Good cornering technique makes training safer and saves time during triathlon competitions. It is a question here of overcoming centrifugal force (F_C) so as not to be carried out of the bend.

$$F_C = \frac{m \times s^2}{r}$$

m = the combined mass of rider and machine.
s = the cornering speed.
r = the radius of the bend.

The larger the radius of the bend (ie the "straighter" the course), the less the centrifugal force and the faster the corner can be taken. However, cutting corners to

"Honking" – the cycle is tilted while the body remains upright.

increase the effective radius is only safe in competitions or on closed roads.

The centrifugal force increases by the square of the cornering speed. You should brake gently before entering the bend. The tyres hold the road badly on corners, so braking then can lead to a crash. Take care especially when cornering on a wet surface.

The centrifugal force also increases with the weight of the rider. You should counteract this by leaning into the bend so as to displace the weight inwards (see drawings right). You should also put more weight on the back wheel by moving backwards on the saddle. Keep the inside pedal up throughout the bend.

Dealing with obstacles

Triathlon competitions are normally planned to include a near-perfect cycling course. But there will still be occasions during training when you come across unforeseen obstacles at speed such as stones or potholes that you have no time to avoid. In order to deal with such situations, you must learn to jump the bike without losing control over the machine.

The front wheel can be lifted by pulling the bars up suddenly with the pedals horizontal. The back wheel can be lifted by leaning forwards over the bars and pulling up with the feet (firmly fixed to the pedals, of course!).
A kerbstone is best for practising on.

Cornering position. In principle there are three ways of countering centrifugal force:

1 Lean the body towards the inside of the bend, but don't lean the bike so far.
2 Lean both body and bike at the same angle towards the inside of the bend.
3 Lean the bike towards the inside of the bend, but keep the body upright or even lean it slightly the other way.

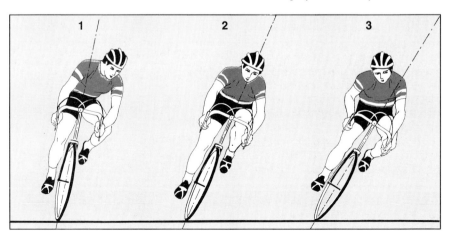

Running

Of the three triathlon disciplines, running is far more subject to stylistic variation than the other two. Physical differences in terms of size, leverage and musculature are just as important in this as individual temperament, running speed and the length of the course. However, there are some points that apply equally to all runners alike, such as achieving a maximum economy of movement and the most effective alternation between muscle tension and relaxation.

Technical description

The action of running can be divided into three phases, best described as take-off, flight and landing. The take-off phase consists of a pushing-off movement that is produced by extending the ankle, knee and hip joints. The size and direction of the pushing-off force is what effectively determines the amount of propulsion, and hence the running speed.

As the toes leave the ground, the runner enters the flight phase, in which both feet are in the air. He then enters the landing phase as the other foot comes down.

The way the foot is placed depends on the running speed: at faster speeds it is the ball or middle of the foot that lands first, while at slower speeds it is the heel. Then the foot is rolled inwards in order to push off again.

From a physiological point of view, landing on the middle part of the foot helps protect the knee and ankle joints,

Running, forming the last section of the triathlon, uses up your final reserves of strength and endurance.

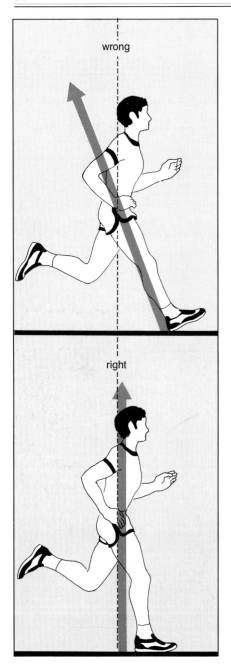

wrong

right

The right and wrong way to place the foot on the ground in relation to the centre of gravity and the mid-line of the body.

take-off phase

flight phase

because there is a certain elasticity that absorbs the force of the impact, which is two to three times the body weight. At slower running speeds it is usually impossible to avoid landing heel-first, because the more upright stance means that the centre of gravity is further back. But at slower speeds the joints are under less stress, so provided there are no orthopaedic problems this technique can be left as it is.

The strides should follow smoothly and should not be too large. The knees should be lifted just enough so that the foot lands either just in front of or immediately below the centre of gravity (see drawings left).

Great economy of movement is achieved by the harmonious coordination of the arms and legs so that they support and reinforce one another. The body should be upright, the eyes looking forward and the shoulders loose and relaxed, while the arms move parallel to the running direction. Ideally the elbows should form an angle of 90°. The hands should be relaxed and slightly open, with the thumbs pointing upwards. You should breathe through the mouth and the nose.

Improvement exercises

Running technique is marked by a high degree of individual variation, so it is sensible only to make corrections to technique when it differs markedly from the accepted ideal. The more miles you cover during training, the more you will

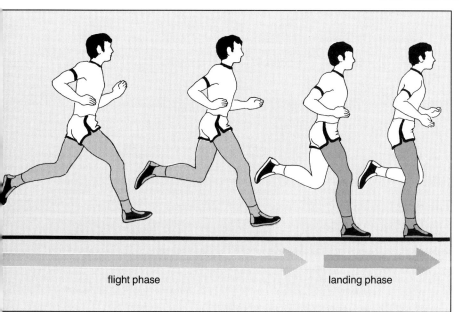

flight phase   landing phase

Left: The different phases of running technique.

Below: The correct arm technique helps the movement of the legs.

hopping movement with your arms.
- Run in jumps, lifting up your knees to create big strides. Push off and land on the ball of each foot.
- Run while deliberately landing on your heels. You will only be able to run very slowly.
- Run in skips, pulling your knees up under you.

be able to develop the style that is best for you. Running uphill, downhill and cross-country will help increase your technical repertoire and improve your ability to adapt to external changes in circumstances.

The technical exercises which follow are all culled from short-distance running. But they can easily be adapted to long-distance running, as the basic movements are the same. Like some of the swimming exercises, they should take the form of contrast exercises, in which uneconomic techniques are replaced by more normal running movements after a short distance of 50–100 m.

- Run in hops, exaggerating the pushing-off movement in the ankle, knee and hip joints, and landing on the ball of each foot. Bend your body slightly forwards, and support the

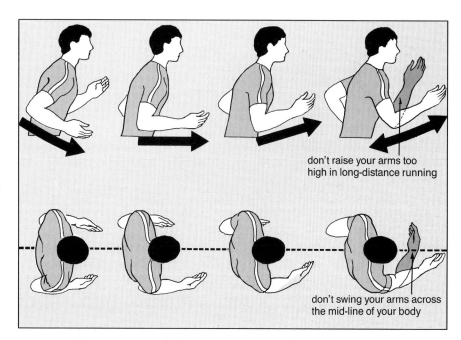

don't raise your arms too high in long-distance running

don't swing your arms across the mid-line of your body

Training

Sports training is the term used to cover all physical methods of improving sporting performance. But it can also involve maintaining performance at the same level – among recreational triathletes, for example. It may even involve reducing the performance level, such as when a former competitive athlete wants to "train down" to a recreational level.

Performance is improved when the body is subjected to a series of specific training loads which stimulate a process of physiological adaptation. The training must be carefully measured according to certain inherent biological laws, which we shall now go on to describe.

Overcompensation

The human body always tries to maintain an internal physiological balance in order to remain healthy and perform effectively. When an athlete trains, this balance is disturbed. His body's energy reserves are used up and he becomes fatigued. During the recovery phase which follows, the body rebuilds the energy reserves it has lost. But it restores them to a higher level than before in a process known as *overcompensation.* The resulting increase in energy reserves means an improvement in performance capacity.

Overcompensation is the basic principle underlying all forms of training to improve performance. New training efforts cause overcompensation, and if repeated will lead to a continual

improvement in performance. However, such improvements can only take place if the training load is specifically geared to the athlete's current performance level. The following equations apply:

training effort too high	>	overtraining results
training effort just right	>	the body adapts and performance improves
training effort too low	>	performance stays the same or deteriorates.

Overcompensation may affect the following areas:

- conditioning (cardiovascular and metabolic systems and musculature)
- technique and coordination (central nervous system, including brain and nerve channels)
- psychology and mental attitude.

The principle of overcompensation.

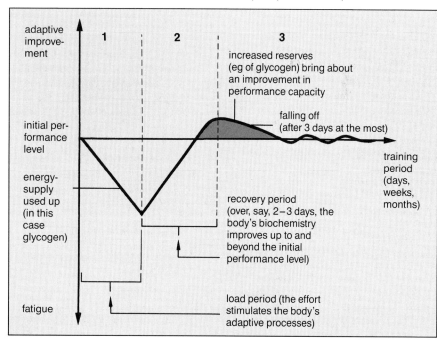

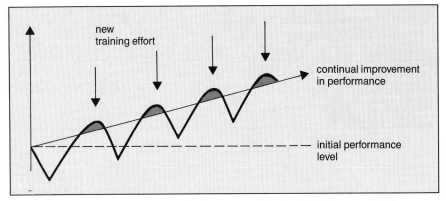

Performance is improved by the most effective pattern of load periods interspersed with recovery periods.

Aspects of physical load

In order to structure the training programme effectively, it is vital to understand the various components of physical load.

Intensity of effort

This term refers to the intensity of a training load, or how much effort the athlete must make in order to carry out a particular exercise.

If the training intensity is so low as to produce less than 30% of maximum performance, then it will be ineffective and will eventually lead to a deterioration in performance. Efforts of between 40% and 70% are considered medium training loads, and lead to a slow but steady improvement in performance.

High-intensity training loads (80–100%) produce a vast improvement in a relatively short time, but the improvement is short-lived and is soon lost after only a short rest from training. Competitive triathletes only train at this intensity over shorter distances during the actual competition period.

The absolute training intensity varies depending on individual best performances; it changes from month to month and from one year to the next. The greater the performance capacity (and the compatibility of the training load), the higher the absolute training intensity and the more difficult it will be to produce further improvements in performance.

When training the cardiovascular system, one must raise the pulse rate to at least 140 bpm in order to stimulate the necessary adaptation processes.

Duration of effort

This refers to the length of time an effort lasts. At high intensities the duration of effort is short. The duration increases with decreasing intensity.

The duration of effort depends on which aspect of conditioning is involved (endurance, strength, speed) and the training method being used. Thus speed exercises are short, while endurance exercises are long, but are shorter in interval training than when using the continuous method.

Volume of training

The total amount of effort, or volume of training, depends on the number of repetitions and the duration of all the efforts that go to make up a training session. The volume of training should be sufficient to produce symptoms of fatigue which then last for a specific period.

The training method and the training intensity are important factors in determining the volume of training. Triathlon training mainly involves relatively large amounts of medium-intensity training.

Density of training

This refers to the proportion of training as opposed to recovery within one session. The higher the training level, the shorter the period between each training effort and the greater the volume of training within one session.

Like the duration and volume of training, the density of training depends on the training objectives and the training method used.

Frequency of training

This term describes the number of training sessions per week, which is dependent on the following factors:

- **The number of years of training** As an athlete trains over the years, he adapts to heavier training loads and the recovery periods become shorter. Beginners, for example, may be able to manage only three sessions a week, more advanced performers six to eight sessions, and high-performance athletes eight to twelve or even more.
- **The quantity and quality of training** The greater the intensity and volume of training in each session, the longer the recovery period that the body requires in order to be sufficiently rested to carry out the next session.

Performance improves in relation to the number of training efforts.

Above: low frequency, therefore only a slight improvement.

Below: high frequency, therefore a considerable improvement.

- **Individual capacity** Different athletes require different training loads in order to reach the same performance level. Thus the exact number of training sessions per week will vary from one performer to another.

The effectiveness of training depends on a sensible alternation between effort and recovery. The regeneration period (that required for complete recovery) will vary from one to three days, depending on the training level and the training load.

If the regeneration period is not observed, or the volume and intensity of training are too great, this will eventually lead to overtraining. Technical training should only be carried out when the body has recovered completely (see page 37). But for general endurance or muscular endurance training, a partial recovery is quite sufficient to prevent overtraining.

Principles of progressive overload

Training must be carried out regularly over a long period to produce a sustained improvement in performance. But this can only be achieved if the metabolic (energy-supply) system and other systems within the body learn to adapt to a higher performance level. An improvement in performance potential must go together with an increase in training load.

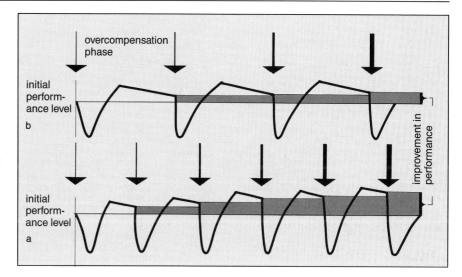

Recovery times and regeneration processes in relation to various training loads

Recovery processes	Aerobic energy supply (running, swimming and cycling)	Mixed aerobic/ anaerobic energy supply (running etc)	Anaerobic alactic and lactic energy supply (speed and strength exercises)	Anabolic effect (maximum strength)	Effects on the neuromuscular system (speed and technique)
continuous regeneration	60–70% training intensity: continuous regeneration				using the interval method with short efforts and long rests
quick recovery (but very much incomplete)		after about 1½–2 hours	after about 2–3 hours		
90–95% recovery (incomplete but with good performancce capacity)	75–90% training intensity: after about 12 hours	after about 12 hours	after about 12–18 hours	after about 18 hours	after about 18 hours
complete recovery of metabolic balance (increased performance capacity)	75–90% training intensity: after about 24–36 hours	after 24–28 hours	after 48–72 hours	after 72–84 hours	after 72 hours

NB Recovery times apply to beginners and intermediate-level athletes. They can be shortened by about 50% for top-level athletes.

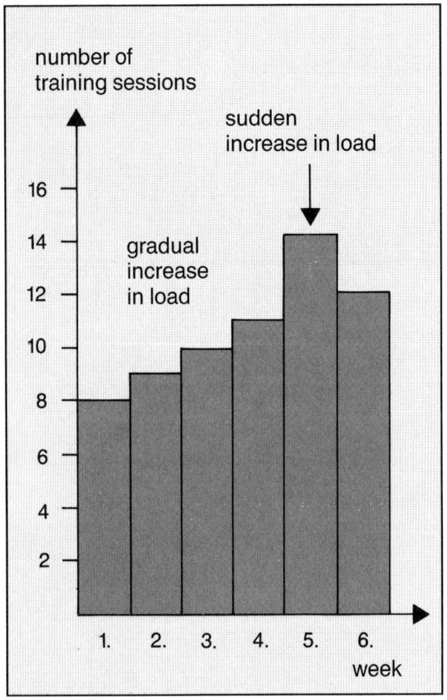

Varied training loads with a gradual and a sudden increase in load.

- An increase in the training load of 20–40% per year represents a gradual increase which should not normally overtax the athlete. This progression is achieved by:
  - training more frequently
  - increasing the volume of training
  - increasing the density and duration of training
  - increasing the training intensity.
- After a certain training level has been reached, it is important to prevent the performance from stagnating. This can be done by suddenly increasing the volume or intensity of training, thus disturbing the internal balance of the body. This sudden increase stimulates the body's systems to adapt to the new load, creating the opportunity for further improvement. However, because the increase is sudden, the recovery period must be long enough to match.
- Monotony in training has a negative effect on motivation and hence on performance. One way of counteracting this is to vary the load. One might, for example, alternate between sudden and gradual increases in load. Using various training methods and training courses will also provide further physical and mental stimulation.

Long-term training

Top performances in any sport are only possible nowadays if the necessary foundations have been laid during the formative years. Long-term training is needed, consisting of up to fifteen years of systematic and single-minded preparation. It begins with an early period of more varied training, and leads eventually to specialised training in the sport or discipline concerned.

Basic training

Experience in other sports has shown that early specialisation is a hindrance rather than a help towards later sporting achievements. Basic training therefore includes a great variety of sporting activities, in which performance requirements are very general and techniques are only taught at a fairly rudimentary level.

Sports performance depends increasingly on mental abilities too, such as the capacity to think and act independently. Such abilities should be encouraged and developed from the very beginning. The same applies to certain character traits such as single-mindedness, decisiveness, initiative, discipline and self-control.

Build-up training

Varied and general training is important at this stage too. But there is a slow progression towards specialisation in that particular encouragement is given in those skills that are particularly vital to the chosen sport.

Competitive and high-performance training

The third phase of the long-term training programme is geared specifically towards achieving the best possible performance. Training is both intensive and specialised, and is geared to producing the best in all areas of performance – conditioning, technique, tactics and mental ability.

The age at which basic training should begin varies, depending on the physical characteristics that are vital to performance in the particular sport concerned. The lowest starting age is five (if flexibility is important), while the highest is fourteen (in sports requiring maximum strength). The triathlon is one of those sports in which endurance comes very much to the fore. In such sports the high-performance phase begins extremely late on.

It is not necessary to begin specific triathlon training during childhood. The best basis for later achievements is a broad and varied programme that concentrates on general fitness and coordination. All three disciplines that make up the triathlon form a natural part of children's normal behaviour.

A sample training programme for the triathlon

The training programme is divided into four phases:

Phase 1 (10–14) — the triathlon as an adventure

Phase 2 (15–18) — basic triathlon training

Phase 3 (19–22) — build-up training in the triathlon

Phase 4 (23–28/30) — high-performance training: Triathlon I
(30 onwards) — high-performance training: Triathlon II

Phase 1 (10–14)

Objectives: to create the basic level of fitness, coordination and motivation that will be needed for later systematic training in the triathlon.

- The development of general fitness and coordination during sport and PE lessons at school (following the principle of variety).
- Training (including competitions) in various sports according to interest and preference.
- General experience of swimming, cycling and running as everyday activities/learning the crawl stroke at school or at the local pool.
- Experience of the triathlon as an adventure sport in a few "friendly" events over very short distances.
- **No** championships, and **no** class or age-group competitions.
- **No** systematic endurance training.

Phase 2 (15–18)

Objectives: to develop aerobic endurance capacity and to introduce the sport of cycle racing.

- Developing aerobic endurance capacity by swimming, cycling and running in the area of the aerobic threshold.
- A slow increase in the volume of training, always avoiding intensive efforts.
- Improving the crawl stroke.
- Introduction to cycle racing at high pedalling rates.
- First competitions over shorter distances.

Training levels in relation to age and physical characteristics

| Training levels | Training period in years | Training sessions per week | Components of conditioning and recommended ages | | | | | | | | |
			maximum strength	muscular power (anaerobic)	muscular endurance (aerobic)	aerobic endurance	anaerobic endurance (>4mmol/1)	speed of reaction	maximum speed	speed endurance	flexibility
basic training (beginners' level)	2–4 years	3–4 times	14–15	10–13/14	12–14	8–12	12–14/15	8–12	10–13	10–13	5–8
build-up training (advanced level)	2–4 years	4–8 times	16–18	14–16	16–18	13–16	15–17	13–16	13/14–16	13/14–16	9–12
competitive training (expert level)	2–3 years	6–10 times	18–20	17–18	18–19	16/17–18	17/18–19	16/17–18	17–18	17–18	13–15
high-performance training (top athletes)	after about 6–9 years	8–22 times	20 onwards	18/19 onwards	19/20 onwards	18 onwards	20 onwards	18/19 onwards	18/19 onwards	18 onwards	18 onwards

- General endurance training in a team sport such as basketball, football or handball.
- Participation (including competitions) in a second sport that requires coordination and helps develop speed and speed endurance (eg team sports, badminton, tennis).
- Frequent transitional periods (holidays) but no competition period.
- A small but slowly increasing proportion (10–25%) of specific triathlon training (combined training and training at competition intensities).

Phase 3 (19–22)

Objectives: the further development of aerobic endurance capacity; metabolic training geared specifically to the triathlon; improvement of triathlon techniques.

- Developing aerobic endurance capacity by swimming, cycling and running in the area of the aerobic threshold.
- Developing aerobic-anaerobic endurance capacity by running in the area of the aerobic-anaerobic threshold.
- Specific metabolic or "over distance" training in cycling and running, to accustom the body to burning up more fat reserves at low to medium training intensities.
- Improving cycle-racing technique.
- Improving crawl technique in ways specific to the triathlon (eg two legstrokes for every pair of armstrokes, breathing once every three strokes, swimming through waves and with a handicap).
- Short triathlon competitions.
- Only a small number of competitions (2–3 major events per season and

4–6 build-up competitions of which 2 at most are triathlons).
- General endurance training in a team sport.
- Further participation in a second sport such as badminton or tennis.
- Periodisation planned around the preparation periods, with no actual competition period.
- A marked increase in the proportion (25–40%) of specific triathlon training (combined training) and training at competition intensities.

Phase 4: Triathlon I (23–28/30)

Objectives: maintaining aerobic endurance capacity during the competition season; further development of the aerobic endurance capacity in winter training; specific metabolic training with reference to individual overcompensation; improvement of specific triathlon techniques in various conditions (eg hot, cold and windy weather); development of stamina and toughness in competitions.

- Developing aerobic endurance capacity by swimming, cycling and running above the aerobic threshold (in the winter).
- Maintaining the level of aerobic endurance capacity by swimming, cycling and running in the area of the aerobic threshold (recovery training sessions in the summer).
- Specific metabolic training at competition intensities during the first part of the competition season.
- Improving specific triathlon techniques in various conditions.
- Frequent competitions during the competition season proper (mid-June to mid-September), with events almost every weekend.
- Competitions divided into three

categories: major events, build-up events and training events.
- General endurance training in a team sport (in the winter).
- Further participation in a second (compensating) sport.
- Periodisation planned around the competition period and the individual athlete's programme of major events.
- A high proportion (70–75%) of specific triathlon training from the early spring through to the start of the competition season, with the other 25–30% devoted to regeneration training.
- Increased specialisation in the short and middle triathlons (specialisation in the middle triathlon is usually only recommended during the second half of Triathlon I).
- Mostly competitions and recovery periods during the competition season.

Phase 4: Triathlon II (from 30 onwards)

Triathletes who are better at the middle triathlon should continue the Triathlon I programme while concentrating on the middle triathlon. The training intensity should be reduced while the volume is increased, and there should be fewer competitions.

Triathletes who perform better in the short triathlon should continue the Triathlon I programme, but should reduce both the volume and intensity of training.

An athlete who has followed such a training programme can achieve his best performances in about ten or twelve years. The resulting level is so high that very heavy training and performance loads are needed to consolidate or improve the performance capacity.

Such heavy loads lead eventually

(after 2–6 years) to a fall-off in performance, no doubt as a result of too much physical and mental demand. A long recovery period is then needed. World-class performers in other sports plan long periods of rest from competitions, during which they train at low intensities before later returning to high-performance training.

Planning and periodisation

High performance levels cannot be sustained evenly throughout the year, and it was with this in mind that Matveyev created his first structured training programme for the whole year in 1958. This programme takes full account of the fact that performance capacity is subject to wide seasonal variations due to physical and psychological factors.

The training year is divided into preparation, competition and transition periods according to a system known as *periodisation.* The programme is carefully planned so that the athlete's performance peaks at the exact point in the year when the best performances are required.

Preparation period: performance capacity developed
Competition period: performance capacity maintained
Transition period: temporary loss of form

The triathlon training programme is worked out on the basis of general sports coaching principles, the specific training requirements for swimming, cycling and running, and the needs of each individual athlete. The programme must also take account of the training objectives

(competition placings/long, middle or short triathlon), the time available for training, any strengths and weaknesses in the individual disciplines, and other factors. In short, the training programme is an individual matter.

Preparation period

The preparation period lasts for between five and six months altogether. It can be divided into two parts, the first lasting for three or four months, the second for only one or two months. For top athletes, preparations for the competition season start as early as the late autumn of the previous year.

Part 1 (November/December to March)
The first part of the preparation period is mainly concerned with the development of basic endurance. This forms a stable basis for the hard training that will follow and the stresses of the competition season. The training intensity remains low or medium, while the volume of training is systematically increased.

Other important features are: daily endurance training in swimming, cycling and running; general conditioning in the form of muscular endurance and circuit training; and specific exercises for developing and improving certain techniques such as the crawl stroke.

The weather in winter means that there is more opportunity for running and swimming than for cycling. However, occasional sessions on rollers or on a turbo trainer will ensure that the cycling muscles are kept in trim.

Part 2 (April to May)
The second part of the preparation period consists of specific training geared towards competition. The pace becomes much harder, with the inclusion of fartlek, alternating and interval methods of

training. In some training sessions the intensity is raised to the normal competition level or even above that (recovery periods are carefully calculated accordingly).

Apart from these bouts of tough training, there is one session a week of low-intensity training over a very long distance. The best method is a long run or cycle ride at the weekend over a distance that is almost up to competition length (excepting the long triathlon).

Clothes-changing and tyre-changing drills are also added to the programme, both during exercise and on non-training days. Another specific exercise involves alternating between the disciplines under competition conditions (see below). Some weekend sessions may also include sudden increases in load, leading to marked improvements in performance (see page 58).

Combined training

The triathlon not only makes heavy demands on the heart, circulation, breathing and metabolism. It also places a severe strain on the coordination between the muscles and the central nervous system.

Each of the triathlon disciplines involves a different set of movements, each employing different combinations of muscles. The rhythm also varies, from 50 armstrokes per minute in swimming, to 100 pedal revolutions per minute in cycling, and 120 paces per minute in running. Each movement is repeated thousands of times during training and competition. The monotonous rhythm gradually becomes a habit. But then the race switches from one sport to another; the old rhythm is suddenly interrupted and a new rhythm must be quickly adopted.

Combined training is the means by

which the nerves and muscles can become accustomed to these sudden changes in rhythm. It is normally sufficient to combine just two disciplines at a time. The most difficult change is that between cycling and running, and so preference should be given to combining these two.

The most frequently used combinations are:

- a long, gentle ride followed by a short, hard run
- a short, hard ride followed by a long, gentle run
- a short, hard ride followed by a short, hard run.

Some triathletes never end a cycling session during the second preparation phase without a short run, even if it is for only a mile or two.

Combined training does not have to follow the usual order of swimming, cycling and running. The very act of combining two disciplines helps train the muscles and central nervous system, making them better able to adapt to either of the two changes that take place in the triathlon.

Changing clothes

It is even possible to save time in the transition zone between two parts of the triathlon. Everyone who trains knows that every minute counts – cutting a 1,000 m crawl from 16 min to 15 min, or a 10 km run from 35 min to 34 min.

It is fairly easy to save a minute in the change-over. And yet this ''fourth discipline'' is often neglected in everyday training, even though it is the distinctive feature that marks out the triathlon from all other events.

It is vital to follow a set procedure when changing, however few clothes actually need to be changed. The change-over sequence must become second nature, so that no thinking is required and no problems are likely to occur (this is particularly important given the heavy demands of competitions).

Competition period

The main aim during the competition period is to maintain a reliable best performance. The period starts in mid to late May, with the first triathlon events using open-air swimming pools. It extends right into October, and culminates in the two great world events in Nice and Hawaii.

The first part of the season is made up of training and build-up events, including people's marathons and cycle tours under competition conditions. This provides an opportunity to test one's form, check out new equipment and try out various tactics such as the best combination of intensities in the individual disciplines.

This first period is followed by a three- or four-week break before the main triathlon events. This should be a time of physical and psychological regeneration, in which you can prepare yourself mentally for the forthcoming competitions. There should be an emphasis on regular training at low intensities but in large amounts. Six to twelve weeks after the start of the competition period, the performance should be starting to peak ready for the main events that are about to come.

The number of events to be entered will vary according to the distances chosen and the athlete's individual performance. This in turn will depend on the volume of training, the athlete's age and the number of years he has trained for the triathlon. In the short triathlon, there should be a maximum of ten to fifteen events per year.

The planning of the competition season should take account of the fact that athletes often seem to peak after more than half the events have taken place. The most gruelling events occur at the peak of the season.

Experience in other sports suggests that there is often a fall-off in performance about ten days before the peak performance occurs. After the performance has peaked, further peaks may be achieved at intervals of a week to a fortnight. If the recovery periods are any shorter, peak form is impossible to maintain.

The chapter on competitions includes detailed descriptions of training methods that are to be used during this period, such as tapering and regeneration training.

Transition period

The transition period follows immediately on the last competition. This is a time of active recovery and complete physical and psychological regeneration. Triathlon training should only continue in cases where an athlete has not been fully stretched during the competition season, whether because of injury or for other reasons.

In the meantime, triathletes should take up other sports which benefit the basic motor abilities that tend to be neglected in the triathlon itself, such as speed, reaction time and coordination. Now is the time to analyse performance over the competition season, to assess the effectiveness of the previous year's training methods, and to consider possible improvements for the next competition period.

Attach a cord to the zip on your wetsuit, and fix the other end with velcro to somewhere easily accessible. This will save valuable time in the transition zone following the swim.

A top triathlete's training year

Preparation period
(lasting 5–7 months, from November/December to May)

Part 1
(November/December to March)
Basic training at low intensities, increasing the volume of training systematically. The training sessions should become longer and more frequent until they cover three or four times the anticipated triathlon distance in two sessions per day.

Content
Swimming: continuous training; extensive interval training; technical training; muscular endurance training with paddles and wearing T-shirt and gym-shorts; flexibility training.
Cycling: training on rollers to practise round pedalling technique and to keep the cycling muscles in trim (30–45 min several times a week); occasional weekend rides if the weather is good to maintain a feel for riding and provide some light relief (maximum 2 h).
Running: steady jogging (1–3 h); occasional competitions over 10–25 km (eg winter marathon series).
Other activities: cross-country skiing, muscular endurance and circuit training.

Part 2
(April/May)
Specific training geared towards competition, increasing the intensity within individual training sessions up to and beyond competition level, but increasing the volume of training only slightly.

Content
Swimming: no more muscular endurance training, but more intensive interval training instead; one timed race per week over the anticipated competition distance; flexibility training; very little technical training.
Cycling: regular cycle rides, at low intensities at first (low gears and high pedalling rates) and in increasing amounts; extra cycle training to make up for lack of training in winter months; later variations in tempo, using fartlek or alternating methods.
Running: intensity increased using fartlek or alternating methods, hill runs, minute runs, jogging with tempo variations and interval training on the course; one long-distance run per week (about 3 h at low intensities, for the middle or long triathlon in particular).
Regeneration training: active recovery after heavy training sessions (eg 30 min of relaxed swimming, jogging or roller cycling).
Combined training: twice a week from May onwards, specific training in switching between disciplines under competition conditions (eg a fast ride over 40–60 km, followed by a gentle run over 15–20 km; or a gentle ride over 100–150 km, followed by a fast 10 km run; or a cycle ride using a fast tempo for the last 20 km, followed by fast interval runs on the course (especially for the short triathlon).
Other activities: getting used to cold water; clothes-changing drills (especially for the short triathlon); tyre-changing drills (especially for the middle or long triathlon).

Competition period
(lasting 5 months, from mid to late May until mid-October)
The development and consolidation of peak form.

Content
- Training events: short triathlons or people's marathons; cycle tours under competition conditions; 85% training intensity.
- Build-up events: maximum training intensity 95%.
- Maintaining form: extensive training at medium intensities.
- Tapering: decreasing the training loads in the two weeks leading up to major events, according to individual requirements.
- Major events: 100% training load.
- Regeneration training in between competitions.

Transition period
(lasting 4–6 weeks, from mid-October until mid to late November)
Active recovery to bring about complete physical and psychological regeneration, training according to mood and inclination.

Content
- Compensation sports, especially those which improve speed and coordination.
- General conditioning (circuit training) and gymnastics.
- A small amount of training in individual disciplines, leading to specific training in swimming techniques.

The training year for a competitive amateur

Objectives: participation in a series of short-distance events and in three to five middle triathlon events.

Preparation period
(lasting 3 months, from March to May)

Part 1
(6–8 weeks)
Basic training at low intensities, gradually increasing the volume of training up to

double the anticipated triathlon distances (about 3,000–4,400 m swimming, 120–180 km cycling and 30–40 km running), changing the emphasis each week.

Part 2
(4–6 weeks)

Training geared towards competition, including occasional training sessions at competition speed; participation in people's marathons; long- distance runs once every fortnight; combined training over short distances; swimming in open water and/or cold water; regeneration training after a weekend training session.

Competition period
(lasting 3–4 months, from June to September)

Peak competition season in August (achievement of personal best time over the middle or short triathlon); competitions divided into training, build-up and major events; all events to be raced full-out; 2–3-week rest intervals between all events to allow active recovery.

Transition period
This is normally not included in an amateur's training programme, as the training load in the competition season has not been enough to warrant its inclusion in the programme. Most amateurs take a break until early spring, practising other sports in the meantime.

If you know you have trained well, you can stay easy and relaxed.

Training for the non-competitive triathlete

Non-competitive triathletes are subject to the same biological laws as those at the top, so training must be just as systematic to be effective. But a top athlete aims to win an event, or at least finish near the front, whereas a non-competitive participant simply wants to complete the course, and preferably enjoy the race sufficiently to be looking forward to the next event. In both cases preparation is essential for these aims to be fulfilled, even though the structure of the training is quite different.

Dr van Aaken has laid down a helpful rule for the minimum training requirement for the marathon. He said, "If you run a whole marathon distance (42 km) every week, then you will be in a position to run the same distance in one go." This statement can be easily adapted and applied to the triathlon: if you practise all three disciplines every week, covering the required distance in each case for the event concerned, then you will be able to finish the course.

Detailed training structure

The training programme can be more effectively tuned to individual requirements if the preparation and competition periods are further subdivided into macrocycles, microcycles and individual training sessions.

Each macrocycle (2–6 weeks) can be geared towards a specific purpose. In the triathlon, for example, the emphasis can be varied between individual disciplines (swimming, cycling or running weeks) or between different aspects of all three disciplines, such as technical improvement.

Within the week-long microcycle, the individual training sessions can be organised and graded according to amount and intensity. Such small-scale planning can take account of current form, weather conditions and other relevant factors.

A training session should always consist of a warm-up session, a main session and a warm-down session. The warm-up should last for between ten and twenty minutes, depending on the purpose of the main session; the more

Periodisation plan, showing macrocycles, microcycles and training sessions.

intensive the main session, the brisker the warm-up should be.

The various elements of the main session should be ordered according to the following principles as they apply to the triathlon: technical training before muscular endurance; anaerobic before aerobic endurance training.

The warm-down leads into the recovery period, and should be geared towards accelerating the recovery. This is especially important when there are several training sessions in one day. Ten minutes should be allowed for warm-down.

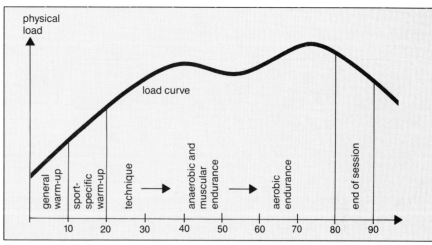

The structure of a training session.

Individual high-performance training

We have now seen how the training year is divided into periods and then further subdivided into macrocycles, microcycles and training sessions. But at the high-performance level such a schema can provide no more than a general plan of action. All the recommended training loads and intensities must be interpreted individually, depending on the athlete's physical characteristics and on the relative effectiveness of the various training methods in his case.

In 1978 Bondarcuk introduced a new training structure which recognises that athletes can be divided into a number of different "response categories", each of which responds differently to the same training efforts. This means in practice that, for example, one athlete responds very quickly to a given training effort, while another needs a much longer time before he responds by adapting to the same effort.

Thus the different stages of the programme can be moved backwards and forwards, depending on the purpose

Special equipment is needed at the high-performance level.

of the training. Only by structuring the training loads on an individual basis can an athlete be certain of achieving his best performance.

One need only look at the physical characteristics of various top triathletes to see a clear differentiation between former swimmers, cyclists and runners and those who have changed over from completely different sports. Then there is the swimmer who is a good runner as well, or the cyclist who can run well but is not such a good swimmer. The number of possible variations can only be worked out mathematically. One important task for sports scientists will be to study these triathletes, whether during a typical period of their careers or from their annual training programmes, and to try to discover a pattern in all this variation that will be of help in planning training programmes in future.

Sample training programme from Jürgen Zäck (2nd in Short Triathlon, 1986 European Championships)

Preparation period part 1: November to February inclusive

	Swimming				Cycling				Running				Other training (strength/conditioning, gymnastics, skiing etc)
	time of day	km	duration	training method	time of day	km	duration	training method	time of day	km	duration	training method	
Mon	20.30	2	31 min	continuous					17.00	18	1:08 h	continuous	12.00 gymnastics pulley rope (10 x 30 strokes)
Tues	17.30	5.3	2:30 h	interval					12.00	11	38 min	continuous	
Wed	20.00	4.3	2 h	interval					17.00	13	50 min	continuous	12.00 gymnastics pulley rope (10 x 30 strokes)
Thur	17.30	3.8	1:30 h	interval					12.00	7.5	28 min	continuous	
Fri	17.30	4.6	1:30 h	interval & continuous					12.00	11	38 min	continuous	
Sat	16.00	1.4	1 h	interval (intensive)	9.30	56	2 h	continuous					
Sun	15.30	2	31 min	continuous	9.30	60	2:05 h	continuous	14.30	14	1 h	continuous	gymnastics

Preparation period part 2: March to mid-May (continued opposite)

	Swimming				Cycling				Running				Other training
Mon	19.00	2	30:30 min	continuous	17.00	65	2 h	continuous & interval	12.00	11	38 min	continuous	12.00 gymnastics
Tues	17.30	4.4	1:30 h	interval					12.00	11	37:30 min	continuous	
Wed	20.00	4.1	1:30 h	interval (intensive)	17.00	48	1:30 h	continuous	12.00	9	33 min	continuous	

Preparation period part 2: (continued)

	Swimming				Cycling				Running				Other training (strength/conditioning, gymnastics, skiing etc)
	time of day	km	duration	training method	time of day	km	duration	training method	time of day	km	duration	training method	
Thur	13.00	2.5	38 min	continuous	16.20	55	1:50 h	continuous, leading into run		7.5	30 min	continuous	
Fri	17.30	4	1:30 h	interval & continuous, sprints					12.00	11	37:30 min	continuous	
Sat	16.00	3.7	1 h	interval	10.00	70	2:10 h	continuous, sprints					
Sun					9.00	100	3:20 h	continuous	16.30	15		stepped-up interval runs on the track	gymnastics

Competition period: end of May to October

	Swimming				Cycling				Running				Other
Mon	8.30	2.2	45 min	interval	15.00	60	1:55 h	continuous					
Tues	10.45	1	15:40 min	continuous, relaxed	9.00	50	1:40 h	continuous	17.00	11.5		stepped-up interval runs	
Wed	8.30	2.1	45 min	interval	14.30	70		continuous & interval leading into run		3	11 min	intensive, controlled run	gymnastics
Thur	8.30	2	40 min	continuous & interval					19.00	14	1 h	continuous	
Fri									16.00	7	32 min	continuous, relaxed	
Sat	competition at 14.00 (1.5/40/10 km); 20 min of relaxed cycling at 9.30 & 17.00												
Sun					11.00	50	1:55 h	continuous relaxed					

Sample training programme from Alexandra Kremer

Preparation period part 1: November to March inclusive

Day	Swimming				Cycling				Running				Other training (strength/conditioning, gymnastics, skiing etc)
	time of day	km	duration	training method	time of day	km	duration	training method	time of day	km	duration	training method	
Mon	16.00	1.5	30 min	interval: 10 x 100 every 2 min					10.00	18	1:25 h	continuous	gymnastics
Tues	15.00	2.2	45 min	interval	19.00		30 min	on rollers	10.00	14.5	1:20 h	interval: 5.5 km start; 5 x 700 m every 4 min; 5.5 km finish	gymnastics
Wed	14.00	2	40 min	interval	19.00		45 min	on rollers, alternating: 5 min intense, 5 min relaxed					gymnastics
Thur									10.00	27	2:20 h	continuous	gymnastics
Fri	12.00	2	40 min	interval	10.00		35 min	on rollers					
Sat							30 min	on rollers	10.00	10	48 min	continuous, leading into cycling	gymnastics pulley rope (10 x 30 strokes)
Sun									10.00	23	1:50 h	continuous	gymnastics pulley rope (10 x 30 strokes)

Preparation period part 2: April & May (continued opposite)

Day	time of day	km	duration	training method	time of day	km	duration	training method	time of day	km	duration	training method	Other
Mon	10.00	2	35 min	continuous									gymnastics
Tues	16.00	1.5	30 min	interval			45 min	on rollers	10.00	14.5	1:20 h	interval, leading into cycling	
Wed					10.00	60	2:05 h	continuous	17.00	10	46 min	continuous	gymnastics

Preparation period part 2: (continued)

	Swimming				Cycling				Running				Other training (strength/conditioning, gymnastics, skiing etc)
	time of day	km	duration	training method	time of day	km	duration	training method	time of day	km	duration	training method	
Thur	10.00	2.2	45 min	interval	16.00	50	1:40 h	continuous					
Fri					10.00	50	1:45 h	continuous	18.00	21	1:37 h	continuous	gymnastics
Sat	15.00	1.1	20 min	continuous					10.00	21	1:42 h	continuous	
Sun					8.00	100	3:40 h	continuous					gymnastics

Competition period: June to October

	time of day	km	duration	training method	time of day	km	duration	training method	time of day	km	duration	training method	Other training
Mon	10.00	2.5	44:22 min	continuous, relaxed					18.00	15.5	1:10 h	continuous	
Tues	7.00	1.2	20 min	continuous	15.00	85	3 h	continuous					
Wed									18.00	12	1 h	continuous	gymnastics
Thur	18.00	1.2	20 min	interval	15.00	50	1:45 h	continuous	7.00	10	56 min	alternating, with short sections at competition speed	
Fri													gymnastics
Sat	German Championships at Roth (2.5/99/25 km)												
Sun	10.00	1.4	24 min	continuous					19.00	10	56 min		gymnastics

Sample training programme from Otto Hoter

Preparation period part 1: November to January inclusive

	Swimming				Cycling				Running				Other training (strength/conditioning, gymnastics, skiing etc)
	time of day	km	duration	training method	time of day	km	duration	training method	time of day	km	duration	training method	
Mon	19.30	2.9	1:15 h	interval					14.00	24	1:40 h	continuous	
Tues													
Wed	17.30	2	1:15 h						14.30	27	1:55 h	relaxed jog, with 7 fast runs over 300 m	
Thur									10.30	12	55 min	continuous	
Fri	18.00	1.7	45 min	interval					14.20	17	1:14 h	continuous	1 h gymnastics
Sat									13.00	5	25 min	continuous, relaxed	
Sun									11.30	16	1:00 h	interval: 2 km start; 3 x 4 km (90%); 2 km end	

Preparation period part 2: February to April inclusive (continued opposite)

	time of day	km	duration	training method	time of day	km	duration	training method	time of day	km	duration	training method	
Mon	17.30	3.3	1:15 h	interval									
Tues	17.20	3.7	1:25 h	interval	8.30	110	4 h	mountainous route	14.00	17	1:09 h	continuous	
Wed					12.00	100	3:45 h	mountainous route	16.25	17	1:11 h	continuous	

Preparation period part 2: (continued)

	Swimming				Cycling				Running				Other training (strength/conditioning, gymnastics, skiing etc)
	time of day	km	duration	training method	time of day	km	duration	training method	time of day	km	duration	training method	
Thur					12.30	100	3:20 h	continuous, level route	8.20	18	1:24 h	interval: 4 km start; 5 x 850 m; 4 km end	
Fri	19.30	2.7	1 h	interval									
Sat									20.00	11	1 h	continuous, relaxed	
Sun					11.40	100	3:30 h	continuous, relaxed	19.45	30	2:05 h	continuous	

Competition period: May to October

	time of day	km	duration	training method	time of day	km	duration	training method	time of day	km	duration	training method	
Mon													
Tues	18.00	2.6	50 min	interval	10.45	125	3:48 h	moderately hilly route	7.15 / 16.50	8 / 8	40 min / 34 min	continuous	
Wed					12.00	108	3:30 h	continuous	17.00	10	42 min	interval: 4 km start; 3 x 2 km (90%)	
Thur	15.30	3	50 min	interval					11.00	24	1:43 h	continuous	
Fri	19.30	2.9	1 h	interval	10.30	140	4:40 h	mountainous route					
Sat													
Sun					competition (1.2/46.4/11)								

Jürgen Zäck's swimming training week during part 1 of the preparation period

Day	Training method	Training distance	Content of training
Mon	continuous	2,000 m (31 min)	
Tues	interval	5,300 m	200 m warm-up swim 10 x 50 m DB/Bk every 1 min 10 x 50 m Br/C every 1 min 10 x 400 m C every 6:30 min 100 m warm-down swim
Wed	interval	4,300 m	400 m warm-up swim 10 x 50 m CL every 1 min 15 x 100 m C every 1:45 min 200 m relaxed 30 x 50 m C with paddles/pullbuoy every 1:00/0:50/0:45 min 200 m warm-downswim
Thurs	interval	3,800 m	800 m warm-up swim 10 x 100 m C every 2 min, intensive 200 m Bk, relaxed 10 x 50 m C every 1 min 10 x 25 m C technique 10 x 25 m DB every 0:30 min 4 x 100 m C every 3 min, intensive 400 m M, alternating every 25 m, to warm down
Fri	interval & continuous	4,600 m	400 m warm-up swim 8 x 200 m C every 3:30 min 2,000 m C in 29 min 100 m relaxed 4 x 100 m every 3 min, each with 5 rest intervals after every 20 m 100 m warm-down swim
Sat	interval	1,400 m	600 m warm-up swim 4 x 25 m C then 2 x 50 m C then 1 x 100 m C every 2 min 1 x 200 m C after 4 min 1 x 100 m C then 2 x 50 m C then 4 x 25 m every 2 min
Sun	continuous	2,000 m (31 min)	–

DB = dolphin butterfly
Bk = backstroke
Br = breast stroke
C = crawl
M = medley
CL = crawl leg-stroke

"every" means that the given distance is repeated after the time shown – eg "10 x 50 m every 1 min" means 10 distances of 50 m, with each distance starting exactly 1 min after the previous one.

Examples from part two of Jürgen Zäck's preparation period

Cycling intervals: 65 km in 2 h
40 min warm-up ride
(gears 42:19–17)
6 efforts lasting 6 min apiece
(gears 52:17–15)
pedalling rate 100–110
interspersed with 4 min recovery rides
(gears 42:19–17)
20 min warm-down

Running intervals: 15 km
5 km warm-up run
gymnastics
4 stepped-up interval runs
4 × 1,000 m along the course
(progressively faster 3:05–2:52 min)
interspersed with 3 min (400 m) recovery runs
3 km warm-down

Combined training:
Preparation period:
55 km cycling in 1:50 h, then 7.5 km swimming in 30 min
Competition period:
70 km cycling with intervals, then 3 km running (each km to be run in 3:20 min, 3:40 min and 4:00 min respectively)

Endurance training

Endurance may be defined as the capacity to sustain a given performance for the longest possible time. It can also be described as the ability to postpone fatigue for as long as possible.

One can differentiate between two types of endurance on the basis of the type of energy supply available. Aerobic endurance is when energy is obtained using available oxygen. Anaerobic endurance is when energy must be obtained in the absence of oxygen.

The degree of oxygen intake or exhaustion can be worked out from the amount of lactic acid in the blood, lactic acid being a by-product of anaerobic metabolism. The lactic-acid level can be measured from a blood sample taken from the earlobe. The energy supply is predominantly aerobic up to a threshold of 2 mmol/l of lactic acid. The value of 4 mmol/l is treated as the so-called aerobic-anaerobic threshold. If the lactic-acid level is higher than that, then performance cannot be sustained for very long.

One can also distinguish between short-term, medium-term and long-term endurance on the basis of how long an effort is sustained.

Physiological adaptation

There are various factors that limit the length of time a performance can be sustained. These so-called performance-limiting factors are the metabolic processes – the processes by which energy is exchanged within the heart, lungs, blood vessels and muscles.

Regular endurance training not only improves the supply of oxygen to the lungs, heart and circulation, it also improves the metabolic processes within the muscles and increases the energy storage capacity. However, performance capacity cannot be increased beyond a certain point, and this is determined by individual genetic factors.

Effects on the heart, breathing and circulation

The **lungs** are where the body absorbs oxygen from the air. Endurance training increases the volume of the lungs and strengthens the breathing muscles. The

Performance-limiting factors in short-, medium- and long-term endurance

Endurance type & duration of effort	Performance-limiting factors
short-term endurance 35 s–2 min	the ability to release large amounts of energy per unit time
	the ability to delay lactic acid production while using the anaerobic energy system
	the ability to continue muscular activity in spite of lactic acid production
medium-term endurance 2–10 min	anaerobic and aerobic energy systems
	maximum oxygen intake capacity
	anaerobic energy capacity
long-term endurance I 10–35 min	aerobic energy system
	maximum oxygen intake capacity (up to 90%)
	glycogen reserves in muscles and liver
	lactic acid tolerance
	the ability to prevent the build-up of lactic acid during effort
long-term endurance II 35–90 min (short triathlon)	aerobic energy system
	glycogen reserves
	20% energy supply from the combustion of free fatty acids
long-term endurance III 90–360 min (middle triathlon)	aerobic energy system
	glycogen reserves
	30–50% energy supply from the combustion of free fatty acids
	sufficient liquid and food supplies after 2½ hours of activity
long-term endurance IV more than 360 min (long triathlon)	energy supply chiefly from the combustion of free fatty acids
	sufficient liquid and food intake

result is that more air is taken in with every breath, and the breathing rate is much lower when the body is at rest. In short, the breathing becomes more efficient.

The **heart** pumps the blood around the body. Endurance training increases the size of the heart. The heart wall becomes thicker and the heart chambers become enlarged. Some top triathletes have been found to have a heart volume of more than 1,200 ml, the normal average being 750–800 ml. A larger heart makes for a greater stroke volume and improved oxygen intake in the lungs. The heart works more efficiently when the body is at rest. Heart rates as low as 40 bpm and stroke volumes of more than 100 ml are by no means rare.

The **blood** transports the oxygen to the cells of the body. Endurance training increases the blood volume, the haemoglobin level (the level of the oxygen-carrying pigment in the red blood cells) and the buffer capacity (the ability to sustain a specific acid-alkali balance).

The **capillaries** are where energy is exchanged between the blood and the muscle cells. During exercise more blood is supplied to the working muscles at the expense of muscles that are not being used. The number of blood capillaries open during endurance training is between 30 and 50 times the number open when the body is at rest. The capillaries also become enlarged. Endurance training has been shown to increase the density of capillaries in the muscles.

Effects on the muscles

Endurance training exhausts the energy stores in the muscles, but when the effort has finished the energy stores are replenished to a higher level than previously (overcompensation). **Glycogen stores** are doubled, while the

fat stores in the muscle cells are also increased. Endurance training also increases the body's capacity to burn fatty acids under heavy training loads, the glycogen stores in our bodies being limited.

Endurance training also changes the composition of the **muscle fibres.** Muscle fibres can be divided into two main types: fast-twitch (FT) fibres, which are white, and slow-twitch (ST) fibres, which are red. Appropriate training brings about an increase in the volume and development of ST fibres. ST fibres are full of certain enzymes that are vital to aerobic energy supply. They are characterised by a high density of mitochondria – the powerhouses of the muscle cells in which aerobic metabolism takes place.

Training methods

Endurance can be improved in various different ways. Each method has a different effect on the metabolic systems of the body. There are three basic categories of endurance training. They are known as continuous methods, interval methods and competition methods.

Continuous methods

Continuous methods are the best way of improving general aerobic endurance. They involve a long period of exercise that is uninterrupted by rests.

There are three different kinds of

Continuous training: exercise unbroken by rests

Constant method	Alternating method	Fartlek method
no changes in tempo	systematic changes in intensity	individual changes in intensity
intensity of effort:	low to medium load pulse 130–170 bpm	
duration of effort:	30 min to 50–120 min	

continuous method. The **constant method** is so called because the tempo is always the same. The tempo is varied in both the **alternating method** (planned, systematic changes in intensity) and in the **fartlek method** (changes in speed according to individual whim).

Training should be for at least 30 min at first, and later for 50–120 min or even longer (on long runs and cycle rides). The training intensity should be considerably

Examples of continuous training
Constant method:
2,000 m continuous swimming at constant speed using competition stroke

Alternating method:
- warm-up ride: 15 min, relaxed tempo, low gears, fast pedalling
- main session: 10 repetitions
  1 min slow: large chainwheel (gears 52:16/15)
  1 min fast: large chainwheel (gears 52:16/15)
  1 min slow: small chainwheel (gears 42:16)
  1 min fast: small chainwheel (gears 42:16)
- 15 min relaxed warm-down

Fartlek method:
60 min jog over undulating course:
10 min relaxed warm-up, then running fast uphill and slow downhill

below competition level. The pulse rate during exercise should lie between 130 and 170 bpm. Continuous methods mainly improve heart function, circulation and metabolism (burning of fatty acids).

Interval methods

Interval training is characterised by a regular alternation between effort and recovery. However, complete recovery is not expected. The new effort is begun during the first third of the recovery phase, when the pulse rate has dropped to 120 bpm.

One can distinguish between short, medium and long intervals on the basis of the duration of the individual efforts. **Short intervals** last for between 15 s and 120 s, and are repeated 10–15 times. The rest interval is incomplete. In **extensive interval training** (60–80% intensity) the rest interval lasts for

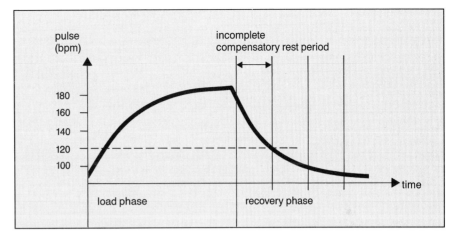

The compensatory rest period.

between 15 s and 90 s (always checking the pulse). In **intensive interval** training (80–90% intensity) the rest interval lasts for 30–180 s. In triathlon training short intervals are used only in swimming.

Medium and **long intervals** are preferred for cycling and running. The longer the efforts, the lower the intensity and the smaller the number of repetitions (6–8 repetitions for efforts lasting 2–8 min).

Pulse rates may rise to 170/180 bpm or more during interval training. The rest intervals mean that a higher overall training load is possible than with continuous methods.

Competition methods

Endurance can also be improved by a carefully planned series of minor competitions. The main prerequisites are a sufficient basis of aerobic endurance and the appropriate recovery periods in between. If the distances are shorter than in the major event planned, then the tempo should be faster than the planned

Examples of interval training

Short intervals:
- warm-up swim: 500 m, relaxed tempo, using any stroke
- main session:
  6 x 150 m crawl (30 s rest, 60%)
  9 x 100 m crawl (30 s rest, 70%)
  18 x 50 m crawl (30 s rest, 90%)
- warm-down: 200 m, relaxed tempo, using any stroke

Medium intervals:
- warm-up run: 20 min with gymnastics
- main session: 6 x 1,000 m (90 s rest, 80%)
- 10 min warm-down

Long intervals:
- warm-up ride: 10 km, low gear, fast pedalling
- main session: 4 x 15 min (10 km), interspersed with 3 min recovery rides (spinning)
- warm-down: 10 km, as for warm-up

Interval training: efforts interspersed with rests

	Short intervals	Medium intervals	Long intervals
Intensity of effort	60/80–90% pulse 180	about 80% pulse 180	about 70% pulse 180
Duration of effort	15 s–2 min	2–8 min	8–15 min
Number of repetitions	5–10 (10–40 min swimming)	8–6	4–2
Rests: incomplete, pulse 120 bpm			
Area of application	swimming	swimming cycling running	cycling running

competition speed. If the distances are greater, the intensity should be slightly reduced. There is also an opportunity to test other aspects of the race such as the effectiveness of new equipment and tactics under competition conditions.

Strength training

Strength in sport may be defined as the ability of the body to overcome, counteract or block resistances by means of muscular activity. The muscles involved are the so-called skeletal

Competition is the best test of current form.

muscles, which are under a person's conscious control. Strength is determined by muscle thickness, the composition of the muscle fibres and the coordination between the muscles and the central nervous system. Strength is the most trainable physical characteristic, even more so than endurance. Three types of strength can be distinguished: maximum strength, muscular power and muscular endurance.

The composition of **muscle fibres** in skeletal muscle is as important to strength as to endurance. We have already noted the distinction between white fast-twitch (FT) fibres and red slow-twitch (ST) fibres. ST fibres benefit the aerobic energy supply, because the high level of myoglobin means that work can be sustained over a long period. However, fast-twitch fibres allow for short, sharp bouts of anaerobic activity, so are vital to the development of strength.

Age and sex are both important factors in **strength training capacity.** For strength to be increased through muscle thickening (hypertrophy), there must be a good supply of growth hormone and male sex hormone (testosterone). Strength training is possible from the start of puberty, but it

should not actually begin until X-rays have shown that the bones are fully developed. Only then are the bones sufficiently stable to support the muscles as they are strengthened. Earlier strength training carries a high risk of injury. Strength training works in the same way for women as for men. But the lack of male hormone in women means that their performance improves less. Muscle makes up only 33% of their weight as opposed to 40–45% in men. Thus women's muscles are only 75% as thick as those of men.

Training methods

Swimming and cycling are endurance sports in which strength is also important. Muscular endurance is a key factor in performance, and this in turn is dependent on maximum strength. Extra strength training is fast becoming *the* key factor among top triathletes. Swimming performance in particular relies on training the swimming muscles on land as well as in the water.

Maximum strength training
A brisk warm-up session is followed by 5–8 sequences of strength exercises at

Different types of strength

Type of strength	Definition	Performance-limiting factors
maximum strength	the greatest strength that an athlete is capable of with the muscles fully tensed	muscle-fibre cross-section intramuscular coordination
muscular power (anaerobic)	the ability to overcome resistances in the shortest possible time	maximum strength contraction speed of muscles interplay between muscles
muscular endurance (aerobic)	the ability to resist fatigue over a long period of continuous effort	maximum strength general endurance

an intensity of 75–95% of the current maximum performance level. Depending on the load, each sequence should follow a pyramid structure, starting with five repetitions at 75% and ending with one repetition at 95%. There should be a 1–2 min rest between each sequence.

Example

- procedure: 6 sequences of bench presses at 75% intensity, ie 6 × 5 repetitions with 75 kg = 30 repetitions (given a current maximum strength of 100 kg weight)
- tempo: slow and relaxed (because of the very heavy loads)
- no of sequences: 5–8 (the fewer repetitions, the more sets)
- rests between sets: 1–2 min

Muscular endurance training

One should distinguish here between general muscular endurance and the specific training of the main muscle groups used in swimming, cycling and running. The training intensity is very much lower than in maximum strength training, while the number of sets and repetitions is correspondingly greater. The pages which follow show some typical muscular endurance programmes.

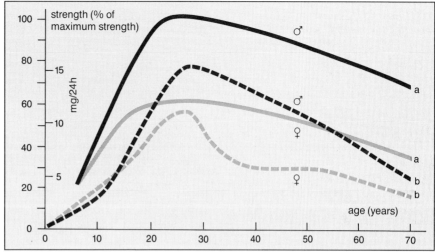

Strength (a) and secretion of sexual hormones (b) according to age and sex. Maximum training values are achievable by women between 20 and 30 and by men around the age of 25.

Cycling is typical of sports requiring muscular endurance.

Stage 8:
Diagonal sit-ups with leg-raise.

Stage 9:
Skipping.

Stage 7:
Raising one arm and the opposite
leg from the stomach position.

Stage 6:
Straddle jump, raising the arms.

Stage 1:
Forward press-ups.

Stage 2:
Squat jumps with arms stretched and feet together.

Circuit training to improve general muscular endurance
- no of stages: 6–12, strengthening arm, leg, stomach and back muscles in turn
- duration of efforts: 20 s for beginners, 40 s for competitive athletes
- rests between stages: 40–80 s for beginners, 20–40 s for competitive athletes
- no of sequences: 2–6
- rests between sequences: 2–4 min

Stage 3:
Jack-knife.

Stage 5:
Press-ups with squats.

Stage 4:
Rocking on the stomach.

Muscular endurance exercises specific to the triathlon
- intensity: 20–50%
- no of repetitions: 10 or more (up to 100)
- no of sequences: 4–10
- rests between sequences: 1 min
- additional equipment: barbell, dumb-bells, foot weights, wall bars

Exercises

1. Lie on your back and hold the barbell in a broad grip, palms upwards and with your arms horizontal above your head. Lift the barbell without bending your elbows until your arms are vertical. Then move back to the original position.

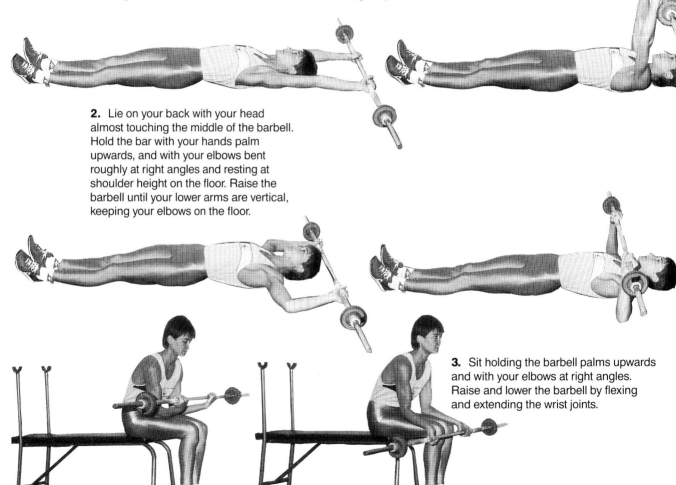

2. Lie on your back with your head almost touching the middle of the barbell. Hold the bar with your hands palm upwards, and with your elbows bent roughly at right angles and resting at shoulder height on the floor. Raise the barbell until your lower arms are vertical, keeping your elbows on the floor.

3. Sit holding the barbell palms upwards and with your elbows at right angles. Raise and lower the barbell by flexing and extending the wrist joints.

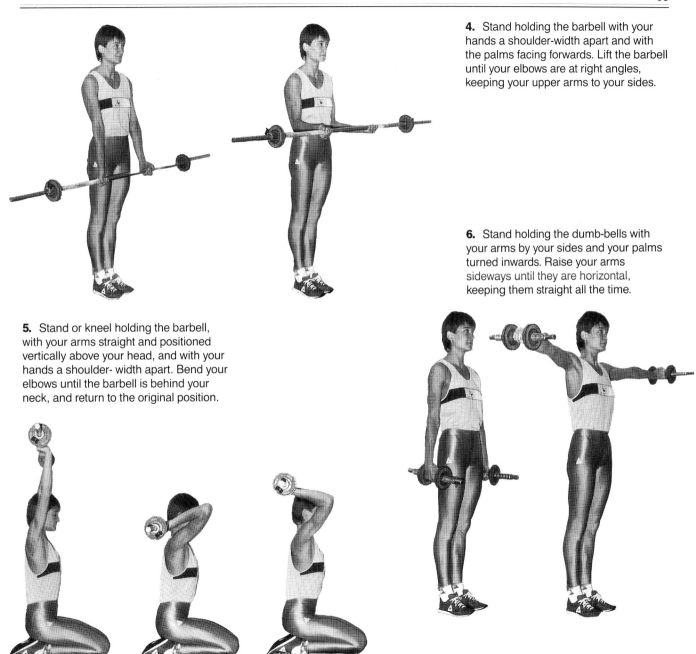

4. Stand holding the barbell with your hands a shoulder-width apart and with the palms facing forwards. Lift the barbell until your elbows are at right angles, keeping your upper arms to your sides.

6. Stand holding the dumb-bells with your arms by your sides and your palms turned inwards. Raise your arms sideways until they are horizontal, keeping them straight all the time.

5. Stand or kneel holding the barbell, with your arms straight and positioned vertically above your head, and with your hands a shoulder- width apart. Bend your elbows until the barbell is behind your neck, and return to the original position.

7. Raise your thighs with your feet weighted, either standing or hanging from the wall bars.

8. Raise your legs while hanging from the wall bars.

10. Straighten your legs against a resistance.

9. Rest the barbell across your shoulders, and jump up and down from a slight knees-bend, making sure that the feet push off vigorously.

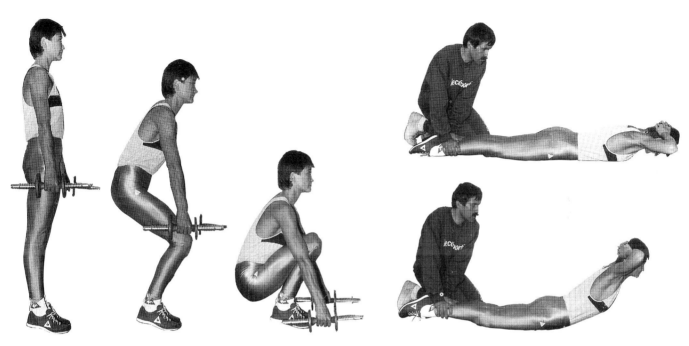

11. Half knees-bends holding the barbell, or full knees-bends holding the dumb-bells.

13. Lie flat on your stomach and raise your upper body off the floor.

12. Bend your knees against a resistance.

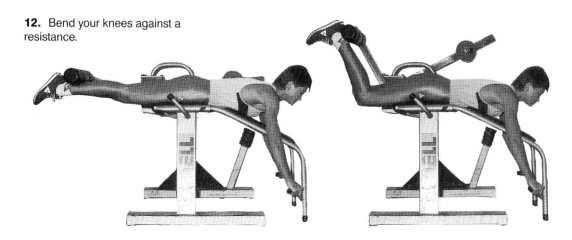

Specific swimming exercises

The muscular endurance exercises which follow are designed to imitate swimming movements as closely as possible. They are intended to train exactly those muscle groups that are used in swimming.

Exercises using a pulley rope

Start from a standing position with your feet together, your arms straight and your hands in the loops. Your position should be just far enough from the point where the rope is fixed (eg wall bars, banisters or a tree) for the two halves of the rope to be just taut when your body is bent forward.

Practise the crawl armstroke as if you were in the water, except that the arms should move together. During the pull phase the arms should pull backwards against the swimming direction until they reach shoulder height. The elbows should be flexed and raised, and should not be straightened until the subsequent push phase. The double armstroke should finish at the point where your hands reach your thighs. The hand and lower arm should be in line, and the hands should be gently splayed as in swimming, not clenched in a fist.

Careful training with a pulley rope can save hours of training in the water. Women are recommended to use a rope with a training load of 10 kg. The load for men may vary between 20 kg and 30 kg, depending on the type and condition of the rope. Sets should include a large number of repetitions (30–50 strokes or more) at a low to medium intensity (the rope should be only just taut).

The body adapts quickly to new training loads as you gradually:

- increase the number of sets (eg from 6 × 40 to 10 × 40 strokes);
- increase the number of repetitions within each set (eg from 10 × 40 to 10 × 50 strokes);
- shorten the rests between sets (eg from 10 × 50 strokes with 2 min rests to 10 × 50 strokes with 1 min rests).

Another tip: wearing cycling gloves saves getting blisters on your hands when training with a pulley rope.

The main muscle groups used in swimming, cycling and running, together with the relevant exercises for use in strength (endurance) training

Muscle groups	Swimming	Cycling	Running	Exercises
arm adductors	armstroke: push and pull phases	climbing position		1, 2
arm flexors	armstroke: pull phase	climbing position	static armwork	3
wrist and finger flexors	armstroke: pull and push phases	climbing position		4
arm extensors	armstroke: push phase	climbing position		5
arm abductors	armstroke: swing phase	climbing position	dynamic armwork	6
hip flexors	legstroke: downstroke	pulling the pedal upwards	flight phase	7, 8
hip extensors	legstroke: upstroke	pushing the pedal downwards	landing and take-off phases	9
knee extensors	legstroke: downstroke (kick)	pushing downwards	landing and take-off phases	9, 10, 11
knee flexors		pulling upwards		12, 13
ankle extensors		pulling upwards		
ankle flexors		pushing downwards	landing and take-off phases	9

Training using a pulley rope.

Isokinetic training machines

There are a number of sophisticated machines available to help train the swimming muscles, including Mini-Gym, Collkraft and Swimbench. They are even better than a pulley rope in that they can also imitate the effect of water resistance.

Swimming with paddles

Swimming with paddles increases the effective hand area, so that more strength is required and the affected muscle groups adapt by becoming stronger. The stroke pattern with paddles is very similar to the pattern without them.

Swimming with clothes on

Wearing a sleeveless T-shirt, or close-fitting tights or a leotard, adds to the passive resistance of the water. This slows down the swimmer and means that more strength is needed to maintain the same speed. But there is a disadvantage in that the crawl movements can be adversely affected in newly trained triathletes who have just recently developed their stroke.

Training in other sports

Some endurance sports such as cross-country skiing, rowing and canoeing have a similar load structure to swimming, with a rhythmic alternation between propulsion and recovery phases. Cross-country skiing in particular uses many of the same muscle groups. The two techniques most suited to developing muscular endurance are the diagonal stride and the two-stick push, with or without an intermediate stride.

Flexibility training

Flexibility in sport is determined by the amount of freedom in one or more joints. Flexibility, suppleness or mobility may be defined as the ability to carry out movements through the greatest possible range. Good mobility is a basic requirement for accurate technique in all sports. It makes the movements more efficient and reduces the risk of injury. The amount of flexibility depends on a variety of factors:

The anatomy of the joints

The flexibility of a joint is determined by the amount of play in the joint, the width of the joint capsule, the ligament structure and the length of the muscles working the joint. Specific stretching exercises can be used to lengthen the muscles, tendons, ligaments and surrounding tissues, thus increasing the range of the joint.

Neurophysiological factors

Flexibility is also greatly affected by the interplay between the muscles and the central nervous system. The body contains receptor cells which continually monitor the positions of the joints and the length of the muscles. Apart from the receptors within the joints, there are muscle-stretch receptors (muscle spindles) within the muscle fibres, and tension receptors (Golgi tendon organs) within the tendons linking the muscles to the bones. When a muscle is suddenly stretched, the muscle-stretch receptors send an impulse to the spinal cord, which sends a reflex message back to the muscle, ''ordering'' it to contract and so prevent further stretching.

The tension receptors are able to prevent this reflex contraction (inhibition of the α motoneuron) and so to allow the muscle to be stretched. For this to be possible, however, the muscle must be stretched slowly and with constant pressure over a fairly long period. Stretching exercises lasting 10–20 s and made up of 3–4 repetitions have proved to be effective. The effect of the muscle-stretch receptors can be further reduced if the stretching exercises are preceded by the isometric contraction of the muscle groups involved.

Warm-up

At low temperatures the fluid in the joints becomes more viscous and flexibility is reduced, making injury more likely. Flexibility exercises should therefore be preceded by a vigorous warm-up session lasting at least ten minutes. This raises the body temperature, speeds up the metabolic processes and nerve impulses, and makes the muscles less tight and rigid.

Fatigue

Hard physical work, whether in training or in competition, tires the nervous system and increases the muscle tone. The result is that flexibility is reduced.

Age

Flexibility is greatest in children and becomes less with increasing age.

Mental attitude

Stressful situations tend to raise the muscle tone and reduce flexibility. The one exception to this is the excitement of keen anticipation before a race, which has a positive effect on the muscles and the range of the joints.

Time of day

Flexibility varies enormously depending on the time of day. Flexibility training appears to be most effective between 10.00 and 12.00 in the morning and around 4.00 in the afternoon.

Factors which help flexibility

- muscles, tendons and ligaments that can be easily stretched
- freedom in the joints and wide joint capsules
- external temperatures above 18°C
- vigorous warm-up before training
- low levels of fatigue – either complete rest or an hour's rest after medium efforts
- youthfulness (childhood to adolescence)
- a state of mental calmness or positive anticipation
- the right time of day (not before 10.00 am)

Training tips

Flexibility exercises must be practised regularly over a long period in order to be effective. Training should start with a vigorous warm-up session (running, hopping, skipping, straddle jumps etc) followed by a series of loosening-up exercises. There should be 2–4 sets of these for each part of the body, each set consisting of 10–20 repetitions.

The stretching exercises should be specific, exercising the shoulder, hip and foot joints in that order, and in such a way that they are exercised equally and in alternation. Each exercise must be repeated 3–4 times in order to be effective. Joints should be stretched as far as they will go without strain, and then held in that position for 10–20 s. It is important to carry out each exercise carefully and accurately.

Loosening-up exercises

1. Make circles with your arms, turning first the right arm backwards and forwards and then the left arm.

2. Make circles with your arms, turning both arms backwards and forwards simultaneously.

3. Make circles with your arms, turning one arm forwards and the other arm backwards simultaneously.

4. Bend over and touch your left toe with your right hand, letting your left arm swing backwards and upwards, then do the same the other way round.

5. Bend over so that your torso is horizontal; cross your arms and swing them backwards and upwards in a bouncing motion.

6. Make circles with your torso, pivoting around your hips.

7. Stand on one leg and make a figure of eight with the other.

8. Swing each leg forwards and backwards.

9. Make circles with your feet.

Stretching exercises

1. Hold your lower arms together just above and behind your head. Grasp one elbow with the other hand and pull it across behind your head.

Stretching the latissimus dorsi muscle.

2. Hold your hands together with your arms straight above your head. Pull one arm sideways with the other arm, keeping your body upright.

Stretching the latissimus dorsi muscle.

3. Bend over and lean against the wall (or grasp the wall bars) at hip height with both arms straight. Lower your left and right shoulder alternately.

Stretching the latissimus dorsi and pectoralis major muscles.

4. Raise one arm and place the lower arm against a wall projection or door frame. Lean your body forwards, keeping your torso straight.

Stretching the pectoralis major muscle.

5. Stand with your hands behind your buttocks. Bend over and raise your arms at the same time, keeping your back straight and your stomach muscles tensed.

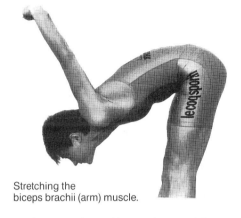

Stretching the biceps brachii (arm) muscle.

6. Sit on the floor with your legs straight. Bring your hands towards your feet and your upper body towards your knees, with your stomach muscles tensed.

Stretching the knee flexor muscles.

7. Sit on the floor with your legs splayed. Keeping your legs straight, grasp your right and left foot alternately with both hands.

Stretching the knee flexor muscles.

8. Lie on your back and swing your leg up towards your head, keeping it straight and keeping your hip on the ground, alternately flexing and stretching your foot.

Stretching the knee flexor muscles.

9. Sit with one leg straight and the other leg bent and crossed over it. Grasp the knee and pull it back towards your body.

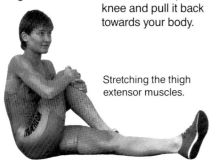

Stretching the thigh extensor muscles.

10. Kneel on the floor and lean backwards, keeping your back straight all the time.

Stretching the thigh extensor muscles.

11. Bring your heel up to your buttock, keeping your body upright.

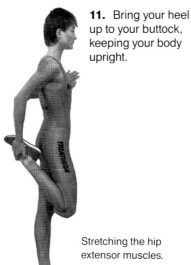

Stretching the hip extensor muscles.

12. Stand about 1 m from the wall. Bring your upper body towards the wall, stepping forwards with one foot, and keeping the other foot with the heel flat on the floor and the toes pointing forwards.

Stretching the calf muscles.

Keeping records

Keeping a training diary is an essential element of training for the triathlon. You should spend just a few minutes at the end of each day, making a systematic record of the training you have done.

A training diary allows you to see exactly how your training is progressing, and provides important information about the effectiveness of your training programme in terms of the methods and structure adopted. Such information will enable you to make sensible decisions about future training.

Every aspect of your programme must be recorded and analysed: the content, volume, duration, intensity and methods of training used; competition and test results; personal details such as weight, resting pulse rate and amounts of sleep; and observations about your general attitude and state of health. Keeping such records is not only an excellent form of self-education, but a vital prerequisite for a successful long-term training programme.

Since the triathlon is a very new sport, there are very few coaches and the majority of triathletes have to work out a training programme for themselves. This makes systematic record-keeping even more essential. All your successes and failures must be regularly analysed, whether in training or competition. You must know why things happen in order to find ways of improving your performance.

During the winter months, when there are usually no competitions, your performance must be tested regularly to check the effectiveness of your training. All you need is a simple regular test, always under identical conditions, such as 1,500 m swimming, 10 km running or 40 km cycling if the weather allows.

Experience has shown that recording methods must be clear, simple and self-explanatory, so that records can be entered and read quickly. We have provided some examples of the kind of diary you might use, but these are no more than guidelines; you should try to work out a system to suit your own needs.

At the end of each season you can record your results on a graph or bar chart. This will provide a more vivid account of your performance over the season.

Surname:			First name:		Summary for the week from				to
Day	Session	Length		Details of training (content, conditions, partners etc)	Weight in kg	Resting pulse on rising	Sleeping time in hours	Comments about general physical state, degree of fatigue/enjoyment
		km	time					
Mon								
Tues								
Wed								
Thur								
Fri								
Sat								
Sun								

	total km	total time	session	time/session	best performance
swimming					
cycling					
running					
others					
total					

Week summary

Week from to	Swimming				Cycling				Running				Other training (strength/conditioning gymnastics, skiing etc)	Comments about physical state, competitions, best performances etc.
	session	km	duration	training method	session	km	duration	training method	session	km	duration	training method		
Mon resting pulse: weight: sleep:														
Tues resting pulse: weight: sleep:														
Wed resting pulse: weight: sleep:														
Thur resting pulse: weight: sleep:														
Fri resting pulse: weight: sleep:														
Sat resting pulse: weight: sleep:														
Sun resting pulse: weight: sleep:														
Total	session	km	time		session	km	time		session	km	time			

Surname:			First name:						Summary for the year from						to

Week	Swimming			Cycling			Running			Total			Weight in kg	Pulse (bpm)	Sleeping time	Comments
	km	time	s/n	km	time	s/n	km	time	s/n	km	time	s/n				
1																
2																
3																
4																
5																
6																
7																
8																
9																
10																
11																
12																
13																
14																
15																
16																
17																
18																
19																
20																
21																
22																
23																
24																
25																
26																
27																
28																
29																
30																
31																
32																
33																
34																
35																
36																
37																
38																
39																
40																
41																
42																
43																
44																
45																
46																
47																
48																
49																
50																
51																
52																

94

Overtraining

If an athlete is subjected to a total training load that is beyond his or her performance capacity and training ability, then overtraining will result. Overtraining is defined as a decrease in performance level during regular training that cannot be attributed to organic illness. Some fatigue is perfectly normal after physical effort, but the amount of fatigue is dependent on the volume and/or intensity of training. Overtraining can be caused by faulty training or by external factors such as lifestyle, environment or health problems.

Overtraining involves changes in the central nervous system, in which the balance between the processes of activation and inhibition is disturbed. Two types of overtraining can be distinguished.

Sympathetic overtraining
This type of overtraining is when the activation processes become overdominant and the body is unable to rest. This happens most often to beginners or undertrained triathletes when they are subjected to high training loads on top of insufficient basic training.

Symptoms of fatigue after different training loads

	Slight fatigue (low training load)	General fatigue (optimum training load)	Extreme fatigue (limits of training)	Symptons of overtraining
Skin colour	slight redness	definite redness	extreme redness or noticeable pallor	pallor lasting for several days
Sweating	light to medium, depending on temperature	heavy sweating	very heavy sweating	night sweats
Technical control	confidently in control	mistakes beginning to occur	very poor coordination and limp technique	limpness and lack of coordination in subsequent training
Concentration	normal	less inclined to listen, less receptive to new techniques and tactical skills	nervous and distracted, with very poor concentration	inattentiveness and inability to correct technique or concentrate mentally
Physical state	no untoward symptoms	muscle weakness, breathing difficulties, debility and decreased performance capacity	painful muscles and joints, with giddiness, nausea and heartburn	sleeping problems, chronic muscle and joint pains, general debility
Motivation	unaffected	less active, inclined to take long rests	desire for complete rest and suspension of training	no desire to resume training next day, indifference and hostility towards the coach's demands
Mood	lively enthusiasm and high spirits	rather subdued, but still in good spirits	spite, aggression and blocking behaviour	continual depression and doubts about the value of training, always finding excuses to stay away

Symptoms that are indicative of overtraining

Sympathetic overtraining	Parasympathetic overtraining
easily tired	abnormally tired
disturbed sleep depressed appetite loss of weight	sleep undisturbed appetite only slightly depressed weight stays constant or vacillates
sweating, night sweats, hot or cold hands	normal temperature
headache, dizziness, heart pains, palpitations, increased resting pulse	heart behaviour unchanged
circulatory tests show a delayed return to the resting pulse after only gentle activity, sometimes with increased blood pressure	circulatory tests show a normal reaction to gentle exercise, but partly atypical reactions to hard efforts, often with increased blood pressure.
low powers of recovery	good, often excellent powers of recovery
inner restlessness, loss of drive, listlessness, depression, discontent	inner calm, moderate loss of drive, normal mood, contentment, indifference

A sense of fun is important too.

This type of overtraining is easy to recognise, as the athlete's behaviour usually becomes noticeably disturbed.

Parasympathetic overtraining
This is the opposite of sympathetic overtraining in that the inhibition processes become overdominant. This condition occurs, for example, after a long period of too much training (usually at high intensity). It mostly affects older, highly trained athletes.

Unlike sympathetic overtraining, it is difficult to recognise as the symptoms tend to remain hidden. The body can still be activated sufficiently to perform, even in difficult circumstances. And performance capacity hardly changes during the long periods of medium effort that most triathlon training is made up of. Only in competitions and in speed tests is there a marked deterioration in performance.

Treatment
Overtraining can be treated by reducing the training load and taking specific measures to enable recovery. Performance tests and competitions should be cancelled. The causes of overtraining should be investigated and dealt with. After the symptoms have subsided, a revised training programme should be introduced slowly, systematically and with great care. The process is often demoralising for the athlete concerned, so specific counselling will be needed in order to restore his self-confidence.

Prevention
The following measures will help to prevent overtraining from occurring in the first place:

- The training programme should be planned thoroughly, with regular training throughout the year.
- Training at high or maximum intensity should never be undertaken until there is a good basis of general endurance. The first phase of the preparation period should preferably be too long rather than too short.
- All hard training efforts should be

Methods of dealing with overtraining

	Sympathetic overtraining	Parasympathetic overtraining
Diet treatment	stimulate the appetite, concentrating on basic foods (milk, vegetables and fruit); reduce protein intake; cut out stimulants such as caffeine; take a course of vitamins, especially B-complex and C; also synthetic preparations such as Multibionta® or Cobidec®	concentrate on acid-producing foods such as meat, cheese, eggs and cereals; vitamin course (B-complex and C)
Physical therapy	open-air swimming; evening baths with additives (pine, hop or valerian extract, or carbon dioxide); cold wash or shower every morning, followed by a brisk rub; relaxing massages; relaxing, rhythmic exercises	contrast baths and contrast showers; medium-heat sauna with several cold showers; stimulating massages; intensive gym work with power exercises
Climate therapy	a short stay in peaceful surroundings (woodlands or mountains), avoiding intense sunlight but allowing a small amount of UV radiation (mountain sunlight)	look for a bracing climate, the sea coast being particularly suitable

followed by a suitable recovery period (see table on page 57).
- The programme should be sensibly structured so that the sports are trained in rotation and the training intensity alternates between high and low.
- The training load should be reduced if there are additional stresses outside (work difficulties, personal problems, climate shock etc).
- Training methods should be continually varied so as to avoid monotony in training.

- A suitable lifestyle should be adopted, including at least seven hours' sleep a night, a regular daily routine, keeping off nicotine and alcohol, and avoiding too much noise or excitement.
- Self-analysis is essential, keeping a diary to monitor training.
- The training load should be increased slowly and systematically after illness or injury. The system can be easily overtaxed, especially after infectious diseases.
- Participation in competitions should be carefully planned and monitored.

- There should be a programme of regular health checks. Information from urine samples and blood tests (preferably taken in the morning) may have important implications for training. For example, rising levels of urea may indicate poor metabolism due to overtraining, while high concentrations of creatine kinase in blood serum are a sign of excessive muscular load. If such symptoms are found, then the training programme can be quickly adjusted on the basis of the measurements obtained.

Competition

Physical preparation

The major triathlon events of the summer season are an unusual part of the year from the competitor's point of view, because they require a specific form of physical preparation. The so-called tapering phase covers about the last fortnight leading up to the event. It involves an individual programme of training to ensure that performance peaks at the right time.

The total training load is reduced, both in volume and intensity. This provides ample opportunity for active recovery from the heavy training of recent weeks, and for building up energy reserves for the forthcoming event. The aim is to taper performance to its absolute maximum. Any mistakes made at this stage can undo all the good work achieved during the months of preparation.

One or two weeks?
There are two important rules for determining the length of the tapering phase. As in other parts of the training programme, their application depends very much on the individual requirements of the athlete.

1. The length of the tapering phase is dependent on the length of the preparation period and the volume of training during that period.

If the preparation period was only very short, or if the volume of training was fairly small, then the tapering phase should be planned to last for one week at the most. If an athlete's form has been achieved in a only short time, it will start to flag very quickly.

However, if an athlete has several months of hard training behind him, then he can afford to allow himself a whole fortnight's tapering with a clear conscience. His endurance capacity is guaranteed by a sound basis of long training, so he can be confident that his form will hold throughout the event at hand.

2. The shorter and more intensive the competition load, the longer the tapering phase can be.

This applies specifically to the short triathlon, in which a top performer can compete at 85–95% of his maximum training intensity in the individual triathlon disciplines. In this case the full two weeks can be allocated for the tapering period.

Put the other way round, the longer the triathlon event, the less the difference on average between competition and training intensities – therefore the longer the training period at competition intensities, and the shorter the tapering period.

The structure of the tapering phase
If the tapering phase lasts a fortnight, then the volume of training should

remain the same for the first week, while the training intensity should be gradually reduced. Bouts of hard training should become sporadic, or no more than a performance test at the end of a session.

Top athletes mostly train hard in the morning and gently in the evening. But as the tapering phase begins, a hard session should be followed by two, and later three, much gentler sessions. In the last 4–5 days before the event, hard training comes in very short bouts, designed to preserve a sense of speed (the exception to this being special training designed to reduce glycogen reserves four days before the event).

The volume of training should not be reduced until the last week before the event. Training should then be systematically reduced from day to day. The following guidelines can be given regarding the weighting of the individual triathlon disciplines:

- An athlete who is equally good at all three sports should run up to three days before the event, cycle up to two days before, and swim right up to the day before the competition itself. This is because running efforts take the longest to recover from, while swimming efforts have a short recuperation period.
- A former runner who finds swimming difficult should rest from swimming for the longest of the three. On the day before the event, an easy 30-minute

Klaus Klaeren: the last week before the 1986 European Short Triathlon Championship

Mon afternoon	60 km cycling (viewing the course) 3,000 m hard swim
Tues morning	45 km test ride at competition speed 5 km hard run
Wed morning	25 km cycling 12 km run
Thur morning	2,500 m hard swim
Fri morning	1 km swim 25 km cycling, including 4 spurts
Sat morning	8 km run, gymnastics and three increases in speed
Sun competition	(1/44/10), 60 min warm-up

Alexandra Kremer: the last fortnight before the 1986 German Championships

Mo	morning evening	105 km cycling (3:40 h) 1,000 m gentle swim (open-air pool)
Tu	morning evening	14.5 km run, including intervals (5 x 700 m every 4 min) 2,600 m swim (including 10 x 100 m every 2 min)
We	morning midday evening	55 km cycling (2 h) 2,000 m swim (including 10 x 50 m every 1 min) 10 km run, medium tempo
Th	morning evening	25 km gentle run (2:02 h) 1,600 m swim (including 5 x 200 m with paddles)
Fr	morning evening	2,700 m swim (2,500 m test at competition speed) 70 km cycling on the Doctors' World Championship Course at Hanau (2:25 h)
Sa	free day	
Su	test event	(1/40/10.5) in 2:11 h, 10 min warm-down swim
Mo	morning evening	2,500 m swim 15.5 km gentle run
Tu	morning evening	1,200 m swim before breakfast (including 10 x 100 m every 2 min) 85 km cycling at Roth (3 h) viewing the course
We	evening	1 h very slow running
Th	morning afternoon evening	10 km slow run before breakfast (50 min) on the competition course 50 km cycling along parts of the course (1:45 h) 1,200 m swim along the Main-Danube Canal
Fr	free day	
Sa	competition	(2.5/99/25) in 5:18 h

jog should be chosen as an alternative to the usual relaxed swim.

■ The same principle applies to the cycling specialist, who should train in his favourite sport on the day before the event, because his body is used to greater training volumes and intensities in this area.

At the start of the tapering phase, top athletes in particular can start to feel uncomfortable as the body is suddenly forced to rest after months of hard training. They may feel ill or their rhythms may be disturbed, producing a feeling of not having trained enough.

There is a growing temptation to insert some extra bouts of hard training into the programme as a test of form. But overtraining is the greatest danger at this stage. If an athlete keeps himself under control, and avoids any unnecessary expenditure of energy, the reward will be an excellent performance on the day.

On the left are two contrasting examples of tapering programmes followed by two top triathletes.

Mental preparation

Apart from the physical preparation (systematic training and tapering), and carefully controlled carbohydrate loading to increase energy reserves, the most important area of pre-competition preparation is the intensive training of the mind.

Motivation

From a psychological point of view, motivation is a vital factor in determining performance. Motivation in turn depends on other related factors, such as:

- innate motivation (not easily influenced);
- the likelihood of success;
- the attractiveness of the goal.

Motivation is best when a goal is perceived as being of moderate difficulty: success is likely but not certain. Training for competitions should include secondary goals along the way, such as training and build-up events of gradually increasing difficulty. The successful achievement of these secondary goals builds up confidence, and thus increasing the motivation to do even better and aim for higher goals.

These secondary goals should be built systematically into the training programme, by introducing tasks of gradually increasing difficulty. Such tasks may include increasing the volume or intensity of training, combined training sessions, swimming in cold water, training on unusual courses, changing a tyre under pressure, and so on.

Often the desire to achieve a specific goal can tap resources that were previously unrealised. Motivation is enhanced if the goal is a very attractive one, such as winning a championship, gaining socially or financially, or simply achieving publicity.

Encouragement from coaches can also be particularly important in the high-performance sphere, because it is in this area especially that athletes encounter conflicts of loyalty. The cost of competitive sport in terms of time, money and effort can run completely counter to personal career aims, whether at school, at college or in professional training.

Motivation problems in training and competition

- listlessness;
- lack of willpower;
- lack of staying power;
- expecting too much of oneself;
- goals set too high or too low;
- unwillingness to take risks;
- euphoria after winning an event;
- dependence on outside stimuli;
- fear of failure;
- crisis of form;
- favouritism;
- too much pressure from outside;
- competition not important;
- competition not stimulating enough;
- high risk of injury;
- rivals much stronger than expected;
- competition reaches a critical stage.

Coping with pressure

There are many obstacles to be overcome on the way to success in the triathlon – heatwaves, cold spells, rain, cold water, demanding courses and lack of organisation. All of these factors add to the mental stresses that an athlete has to cope with. Further stress can be created by other factors such as those listed in the previous section.

There are a number of ways of dealing with these problems. The aim is to create a basic feeling of positive expectation and drive towards the competition at hand. The following techniques have all proved effective in this:

- autogenic training;
- progressive muscular relaxation;
- yoga;
- biofeedback;
- relaxation-activation techniques;
- desensitising techniques.

An athlete is never motivated to achieve his best performances by fear or threats, but only by a challenge that has positive associations. Thoughts of failure or of bad performances are continually

pushed aside and replaced with positive attitudes. The athlete is "psyched up" in such a way as to be geared and motivated towards success.

Mental training, like physical high-performance training, is a long process that is best carried out under the supervision of a psychologist, or of a coach or assistant who is trained in such techniques. Good mental resilience is an important training objective for all high-performance athletes. It is essential in order to survive all the ups and downs of such a career over a long period.

Mental rehearsal

The following information is needed in order to be well prepared for a competition:

- Everything to do with the location where the competition takes place: journey time from home, accommodation, food provision, timetabling, distance between accommodation and competition course etc
- The competition course: choosing the right equipment, gearing, danger points, navigating the swimming course, water temperature, change-over zones, number of refreshment points etc
- Climatic considerations which might make it advisable to arrive early (such as getting used to a hot climate)
- The other competitors: knowledge of their strengths and weaknesses in the various disciplines, and a realistic awareness of your own abilities in relation to theirs, helps you to structure the race effectively from a tactical point of view.

Once you have this information, you should rehearse the whole competition in your mind, concentrating visually on small adjustments that may save seconds. Forget the days when you felt limp and trained badly, and concentrate on all the positive experiences, such as when you improved your personal best time by 30 s on the 1,000 m crawl, or when you first got your bike up a particular climb without any difficulty. Why shouldn't the competition go just as well? After all, your main rival finished his last event only just ahead of someone who is obviously less good than you are!

Many triathletes use such mental rehearsal when preparing for a competition. They think about how they would solve problems that might easily occur, and make decisions that might be difficult to reach objectively in the heat of the race (such as whether to give up or plough on in the case of a puncture or

exhaustion). If you have neglected to do this, then there is a danger that you may give up too soon because fatigue has sapped your motivation, and that you may repeat this scenario in other similar situations. And the lack of success will result in a loss of self-confidence.

Good swimmers have often found, for example, that the longer they can ride before being overtaken by a cycling expert, the more confident they become as a result. They find new reserves of energy – whereas if they only think about being overtaken quickly, their powers are correspondingly frustrated. The same applies to cyclists the other way round.

Once you are aware of the psychological factors that determine performance, you will be part-way

towards learning to control them.

The competition day

There are few sports that require as much equipment as the triathlon. One important part of competition preparation is the task of bringing all the equipment up to scratch, especially the bicycle, which should be checked thoroughly by an expert (many competition organisers provide a cycle maintenance service).

When packing the equipment, allow plenty of time for checking it thoroughly, from the bicycle and running shoes right down to the smallest item that may be essential to the smooth running of the race. The best way to do this is to collect

Competition checklist

Before the event
- starting documents
- tracksuit, plus windproof/waterproof jacket if necessary
- warm socks and gym-shoes or bathing shoes (a lot of heat is lost through the soles)
- waterproof watch
- mineral water (remember to drink a mugful before the start, especially in hot weather or before a middle or long triathlon)
- banana or energy bars in case the last meal was eaten more than three hours earlier
- toilet paper
- sticky tape
- rubber band, transparent envelope, safety pins

For swimming
- triathlon suit or swimsuit/trunks
- neoprene suit if necessary

- one or more bathing caps (a bathing cap bearing the starting number is issued by the competition organisers)
- vaseline (to apply, for example, to areas where the neoprene suit may rub)

For cycling
- bicycle (with the correct gearing), equipped with tyre pump, one or two spare tyres and two "quick bottles" (two spare tyres are often not enough for the long triathlon [eg when it rains]; at the 1985 European Championships at Almere, as many as ten tyre-changes were needed in some cases)
- full drinking bottle in bottle cage
- crash hat
- cycling gloves (recommended for middle and long triathlons, and for short triathlons to avoid unpleasant grazes in a crash)
- cycling shorts and cycling vest with starting number (these are of course unnecessary if you are cycling in a triathlon suit)

- cycling shoes
- sunglasses/suntan lotion
- banana or energy bars taped to the frame

For running
- running shoes with easy-tie laces (do without socks if possible when cycling and running)
- running vest with starting number, if not running in triathlon suit or swim suit/trunks
- white cap with a wide peak to shade the eyes from the sun
- vaseline (the main areas that are liable to rub are the thighs, nipples and armpits)
- sweatband

After the event
- clean dry clothing
- shoes (open sandals or bathing shoes are the most comfortable)
- soap and towel
- mineral water or electrolyte drink, and a high-carbohydrate snack
- massage oil; surgical spirit

everything together before packing, and to check every item against a carefully prepared checklist such as the one shown opposite. You will then avoid any nasty surprises in the last few minutes before the start. Such surprises can easily knock you off balance at that vital moment.

The sequence of events

1. Arrive well in time.
2. Make sure you have your starting documents ready (often to be obtained at a preliminary meeting on the previous day).
3. Divide up the equipment you need for swimming, cycling and running, and pack them in three bags earmarked for each part of the race. Your starting numbers may be secured in several ways:
   - fixed to the front and back of your triathlon suit;
   - fixed to the back of your cycling vest and the front of your running vest;
   - inserted in a transparent envelope and fixed to a rubber band by means of two safety pins, then either worn during the swim or packed in the cycling bag for putting on at the change-over;
   - fixed to the cycle frame.
4. Hand your running bag in at the appropriate place.
5. Take your bicycle together with your cycling bag to the change-over area between the swimming and cycling courses. Check the tyre pressures and inspect the tyres, and set the correct gearing ready for the race. Unless the organisers specify otherwise, you can fix your crash hat, gloves and shoes (with safety pedals) to the bike in readiness.

The cycle park for a major competition.

6. Your starting number is written on your upper arm.
7. Now it is time to start warming up for the swimming start. The warm-up session should last 20-30 min, and finish about 10 min before the start. The effects of warm-up last for 20–30 min, so you should start warming up at least half an hour before the start.

   Start with a gentle jog lasting 10 min, followed by loosening-up exercises and gentle stretching exercises (see pages 88–89). Avoid any type of exercise that you are not used to. Wear sufficiently warm clothing, but not too warm. Thanks to the warm-up you should be fresh and ready for action, not sweating or out of breath, as you move on towards the start.
8. You will need the following equipment for the swimming start: a neoprene suit over the top of your triathlon suit, swim goggles and a bathing cap with your starting number. If the water is very cold, you can pre-warm the neoprene suit by pouring a jugful of warm water into the slit. The goggles can be prevented from misting up (if they are not pretreated) by rubbing a little spittle over the inside.
9. Your position in the starting order should reflect your own performance level. This is the only way to ensure a smooth start without any jostling or painful overtaking manoeuvres. The swimmers either start in the water or dive in from the side.
10. Even swimming is subject to slipstreaming effects. If you swim close to the person in front, you will not only swim faster, but you will not

need to keep lifting your head to see where you are. However, you should be careful not to swim too close. If the person in front signals that you are crowding him, you should respond by allowing him some extra space.

11. As soon as you have left the water, you should unzip your neoprene suit and remove it down to waist level. Take off your goggles and bathing cap. After a sea swim you must always go through a shower, and if necessary wash the sand off your feet in the buckets provided.

12. Now follow your well-practised change-over routine, taking off your neoprene suit and putting on your cycling things, either next to your racing bike or in a specified changing area. You need not bother to dry yourself, and in the short triathlon you may often manage without cycling gloves.

13. If the water was very cold, it is a good idea to ride the first few kilometres in a low gear at a high pedalling rate, and to relax through the effort (shivering from the cold uses up a lot of energy).

14. Sportsmanship is important on the cycling course: take care while overtaking or negotiating bends, and race fairly without crowding the other cyclists.

15. In hot weather, and in the middle or long triathlon, you should drink plenty from the beginning, and eat at regular intervals (see page 116). In hot weather, if the water bottle is not

Starting in the water.

empty by the time you reach the next refreshment point, you should tip the remainder over you to cool off before refilling the bottle.

16. When you reach the end of the ride, you should slow down quickly and hand your bike over to the assistants. During the last few metres you should have loosened your toestraps (if any) and your crash hat and gloves ready to take them off.

17. If the ground is suitable, it is a good idea to leave your cycling shoes and gloves with the bike, or else remove them immediately afterwards and run barefoot into the changing area. On the way you can remove all the other items you won't need for running, and quickly drop them off in the changing area.

18. Use running shoes with a special rucksack-type device that saves unnecessary time tying laces up.

19. In hot or sunny weather, you should always wear a cap to protect your head. Have a drink at every refreshment point, and cool off by pouring water over your head and neck, and maybe over your legs as well.

20. When you have finished, take plenty of time to recover (drinks, fruit and massage services are available). Then collect your bags together and go and fetch your bike.

A quick look at your watch at the end of the swim will tell you if the race is going according to schedule.

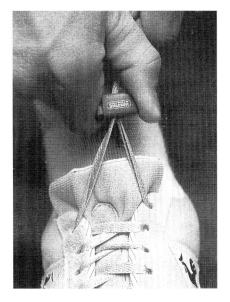

Some running shoes have a special rucksack-type device that saves time putting them on.

The recovery period

A successful performer must be able to recover quickly from an event in order to be in the best possible form for the next one. Energy reserves are depleted after a race; there is an excess of waste products such as lactic acid and urea in the body, while profuse sweating has disturbed the body's water and mineral balance; and muscular fatigue quickly sets in. The first two essentials in order to aid the recovery process are a careful diet and a sufficient supply of fluids.

Diet

Even if you have been totally depleted of energy, you can raise your glycogen reserves to their previous level in only 24 hours by means of a diet that is rich in carbohydrates. If the food is rich in fats and proteins instead, it will take 72 hours before you reach the same glycogen level. Apart from carbohydrates, you should also make sure you have sufficient protein, iron and vitamins in your diet (see page 116).

Fluid intake

When drinking to restore the fluid lost in sweat, it is not advisable to use ordinary tap water. The body needs both water and minerals in the correct proportion, and ordinary water cannot be absorbed if the necessary minerals are missing.

There are a number of electrolyte drinks on the market that contain just the right proportion of minerals for

You must be sure to drink enough during the competition, especially if the weather is very hot.

performers in endurance sports. Another possibility is to drink fruit or vegetable juices that contain vital minerals such as potassium and calcium. Alcoholic drinks are not recommended, not even beer. They slow down the recovery process, and don't contain enough minerals to make up the loss.

Active and passive regeneration

Diet and fluid intake are not enough on their own to ensure a speedy recovery. Other additional measures are recommended such as passive physiotherapy and active recovery.

Passive therapy
The principle of such methods is the use of physical stimuli such as warmth, cold or pressure in order to speed up the recovery processes within the body. Saunas, jacuzzis and massage all stimulate the circulation in the skin, muscles and internal organs. They relax the muscle tension produced by heavy exercise, and speed up the disposal of metabolic wastes.

Active recovery
Gentle exercise as soon as possible after the competition (30 min of swimming, cycling or jogging) helps by increasing the circulation in the affected muscle groups so that the metabolic waste products can be flushed out more speedily. Stretching and loosening-up exercises help to reduce tension more quickly.

Progressive muscular relaxation

Competitions are full of stressful situations that an athlete must deal with, creating a heavy psychological load. But just as the body can adapt to physical efforts, so the mind too can be trained to adapt to all the stresses that it is subjected to, whether in training or in competition.

Research has shown that some of these mental training techniques actually speed up the process of recovery. Examples of these are the various relaxation techniques and strategies for coping with stress. Such methods work best in combination with passive therapeutic measures such as massage, saunas or jacuzzis.

One of the most effective of these techniques is progressive muscular relaxation (PMR). The aim of this method is to bring about an advanced state of relaxation by systematically training each of the various muscle groups so that it can relax of its own accord.

One by one, each muscle group is tensed for about 5–10 s and then relaxed. You work all the way around the body, starting with the hands, the lower arms, the upper arms, forehead, and various face and neck muscles, then working down via the shoulders, the chest, the diaphragm and stomach muscles down to the thighs and calves. You should take special note of the feelings associated with relaxation.

As you become more practised, you will eventually be able to relax whole combinations of muscles, such as all the arm and leg muscles simultaneously. Expert help is needed in order to learn the technique properly. PMR can be employed in a number of different ways in training and competition:

- It can be used to aid recovery during short rests during training.
- Specific muscle groups can be relaxed during exercise to prevent cramps and muscle spasms from developing in training and competition.
- If an athlete is over-activated before a competition, PMR can be used to reduce the activation to more manageable proportions, or else to channel it more effectively.
- When fatigue develops during training or competition, PMR can reduce the effort by helping to regulate movement and make the body work more efficiently.

Medical aspects

Diet and nutrition

One important requirement for success in the triathlon is a healthy diet that fulfils all the body's nutritional needs. Without such a diet a triathlete cannot hope to achieve a good performance level or sustain it for any length of time.

Carbohydrates

Carbohydrates are the most important part of our diet. The simplest, most basic forms of carbohydrate are the so-called monosaccharides, which include fructose (fruit sugar) and glucose (grape sugar).

Glucose is stored in the body in the form of glycogen, and both are vital in the metabolism of carbohydrates. Glucose provides the quickest available form of energy, using up much less oxygen than is required to metabolise fats. Every 100 ml of blood contains 80–120 mg of glucose. This so-called blood-sugar level must be kept constant in order to supply energy to vital organs such as the brain and central nervous system (which relies exclusively on glucose for its energy supply).

Glycogen is stored mainly in the muscles, but also to a certain extent in the liver. Glycogen plays a vital role in performance, especially in endurance sports. The body's glycogen stores can be increased by means of specific training procedures that work according to the same principle as overcompensation. The glycogen stores are completely exhausted through heavy endurance exercises, and are then restored by means of a carbohydrate-rich diet. This process boosts the glycogen in the muscles to a much higher level than previously.

Triathletes (and other endurance athletes) are recommended to follow a diet in which 65–80% of the total energy is supplied from carbohydrate sources. Large amounts of water and potassium are also needed for glycogen formation, so the diet should also include potassium-rich foods and a sufficient supply of fluids. Wholefood-type carbohydrate sources are preferable, as these also contain vital minerals, trace elements and fibre. Examples of these are wholegrain brown rice, wholegrain muesli, wholemeal bread and other wholemeal products, beans, vegetables and fruit. Sugar and refined flour products should be avoided.

Fats

Fats are required for a number of different bodily functions: they are constituents of cell membranes; they afford protection to vital organs such as the kidneys; they insulate the body against heat and cold (subcutaneous tissues); they form pressure pads in the hands and feet; they act as an energy store and as a medium for carrying fat-soluble vitamins; and they are involved in the production of hormones.

Fats are basically composed of triglycerides. A triglyceride is a glycerol base to which three fatty acids are

The importance of different nutrients in food

Nutrients	Why the body needs them
carbohydrates	efficient energy suppliers that economise on oxygen
fats	indigestible energy reserves energy suppliers building materials
proteins	building materials for muscles, enzymes, hormones and antibodies
water	the main constituent of the body transport and disposal of materials in the body temperature regulation
vitamins, minerals, trace elements	control and maintenance of metabolic functions

Different types of carbohydrate

Types of sugar	Examples	Sources	Usability
monosaccharides (simple sugars)	glucose (dextrose, grape sugar) fructose (laevulose, fruit sugar) galactose	honey, fruits, drinks, sweets, milk	sugars that are quickly available
disaccharides (double sugars)	saccharose (sucrose, beet or cane sugar) maltose (malt sugar) lactose (milk sugar)	household sugar, jams, sweets, fizzy drinks, malt beer / milk	digestible sugars that provide energy
oligosaccharides (multiple sugars)	maltotriose maltotetrose maltopentose etc (sugar mixtures) dextrine	special energy drinks for athletes / crispbreads	carbohydrates that are digested over a long period
polysaccharides (complex sugars)	cellulose • amylose • amylopectin (starch)	potatoes, cereals, muesli, bread, pasta, bananas	
	glycogen (animal starch)	liver	
	cellulose lignin pectin	cereal fibre (bran), fruit and vegetables	indigestible carbohydrates

attached. Fats vary according to the particular fatty acids involved (unsaturated, polyunsaturated and saturated fats). Polyunsaturated fatty acids are important nutritionally, especially linoleic acid (5–10 g required daily). A shortage leads to problems in membrane structures and in the production of tissue hormones.

Fats are particularly important as energy suppliers for long-term endurance. More oxygen is needed to metabolise them, but they are practically inexhaustible as energy suppliers. A poorly trained athlete relies almost exclusively on carbohydrates for energy; these are eventually exhausted and he is forced to stop. (The so-called "dead point" in the 30th kilometre of the marathon is none other than the point where carbohydrate reserves are exhausted and fats cannot be metabolised.) But a well-trained athlete is able to metabolise fats as well as carbohydrates from the very beginning, thus economising on carbohydrates. This is because training has stimulated the supply of fat-metabolising enzymes.

A low-fat diet is preferable, with fats accounting for only 15% of total consumption. Vegetable fats and vegetable oils are recommended, including linseed oil, sunflower oil, soya oil and soft margarine. You should not eat foods containing non-visible fats such as meat products, biscuits, cakes, chocolate, mayonnaise, chips etc. Foods containing cholesterol (eg butter) should not be allowed to oxidise, whether by melting or through exposure to the air. This is because oxidised cholesterol causes cell damage in the blood vessels, sometimes leading to hardening of the arteries.

Proteins

Proteins are the basic building blocks of all living cells. They are to be found in muscle fibres, bone structures, tendons and skin; they are also found as constituents of hormones, enzymes etc. Proteins are in turn made up of amino acids. Human chromosomes contain a combination of 22 amino acids, giving each individual a unique protein combination.

The amino acids that we need must be supplied from the proteins in the food we eat. This applies especially to those amino acids that cannot be produced by the body itself (essential amino acids). The quality, or biological value, of food proteins is determined by the proportion of essential amino acids that they contain. The biological value is measured as the number of grams of body protein that can be built up from 100 g of food protein.

High-protein foods include milk and milk products, eggs, pulses (peas, beans and lentils), cereals (wheatgerm), potatoes, rice and nuts. The protein intake for endurance athletes should not exceed 15% of total food intake. This is because surplus protein is turned into extra fat, and the poisonous by-products of protein metabolism place an extra burden on the liver and kidneys. More

Biological values of different protein mixtures for human beings

Protein mixture		Biological value
beans and maize	(52%/48%)	101
milk and wheat	(75%/25%)	105
egg and wheat	(68%/32%)	118
egg and milk	(71%/29%)	122
egg and potato	(35%/65%)	137

Protein content of various foods

Foods	Grams of protein per 100 g of food
meat	up to 21
fish	up to 21
cheese	20 – 30
milk	3 – 4
quark	12 – 17
egg	13
wheatgerm	27 – 28
pulses	23 – 25
bread	6 – 10
potatoes	2
rice	7
nuts	14 – 26
flour products	13

urine is produced, resulting in the loss of water and minerals such as potassium, magnesium and calcium. The overall effect is a reduction in endurance capacity.

Food proteins cannot be stored in the body. So it is a good idea to increase the protein intake either two hours before exercise or up to six hours afterwards.

Water

The body is made up of 60% water. Water plays a vital role, both as a temperature regulator, and as a solvent and transport medium within the body. Two-thirds of our water is contained inside the body cells, and a third outside them.

Physical exercise creates extra body heat, which must be expelled from the body in order to prevent overheating. This is achieved by an increase in the production of sweat, which cools the body by evaporating from the skin. Trained athletes can often produce as much as 2 – 3 litres of sweat. But water loss reduces performance: a loss of only one litre of fluid can lead to a 15% reduction in performance. The faster the fluid loss (eg in hot weather), the greater the reduction in performance.

It is therefore vital to drink enough fluid before, during and after a triathlon event. Water loss produces a thirst, but usually not until enough fluid has already been lost to affect performance. So for long endurance events, and in hot weather especially, thirst must be prevented well before it occurs. The best

Foods which provide extra protein in combination

Cereals with milk
rice, wheat, buckwheat, oats, barley, rye, millet } with milk, cheese, quark, yogurt, sour cream

eg: wholemeal or buckwheat pancakes with milk, muesli with milk or yogurt, wholemeal pasta with cheese, wholemeal bread with cheese, yogurt and wheatgerm etc

Cereals with pulses
rice, wheat, buckwheat, oats, barley, rye, millet } with beans, peas, lentils, soybeans, chickpeas

eg: bean soup with rice, millet with chickpeas, pea soup with wholemeal rolls etc

Cereals with egg
rice, wheat, buckwheat, oats, barley, rye, millet } with egg

eg: buckwheat pancakes with egg, scrambled egg with cereal etc

Potatoes with egg or milk
potatoes with egg, milk, yogurt, quark, sour cream, cheese

eg: jacket potatoes with quark, fried potatoes with fried egg, potatoes baked with cheese etc

NB: The higher amino-acid levels from these foods last for four to six hours, so these food combinations may be eaten over a longer period instead of at the same time.

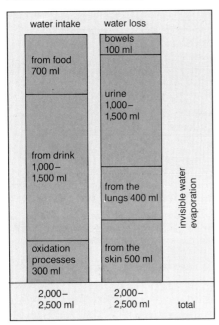

The fluid balance (ml/day) in an untrained adult weighing 70 kg.

recipe is half a litre 15–30 min before the effort begins, a half to one litre during the event (more than is needed to quench thirst) and another half-litre after the race.

Most books recommend mineral drinks during competitions, but this is not advisable because they usually contain too much glucose and minerals (especially sodium). Both of these keep the water in the stomach when it is needed much more urgently in the muscles. The absorption rate for most electrolytes (ie the time taken from its consumption to its actual arrival in the muscles) is much too slow for them to be effective during the actual competition. Ordinary tap water is therefore recommended as being quite sufficient during exercise, provided it is neither too hot nor too cold.

All alcoholic drinks (including beer) are detrimental to endurance capacity. Alcohol prevents the build-up of hormones that slow down water secretion in the kidneys. Thus there is an even greater loss of water and important minerals. The metabolism of alcohol also uses up more vitamins, depleting the body's resources even further.

Vitamins

Vitamins are compounds that act as catalysts, regulating the various metabolic processes within the body. The human body is unable to produce its own vitamins, which (like fatty acids) must be obtained from food. Vitamins can be divided into two main categories: water-soluble and fat-soluble vitamins.

Extra vitamins are needed for sporting activities. Some scientists are now even suggesting that the so-called anti-oxidant vitamins (B_1, B_6, C, E and pantothenic acid) help to slow down the ageing process. Vitamins improve both health and performance, and also speed up some of the healing processes.

Daily vitamin requirements for endurance athletes

- vitamin B_1 6–8 mg;
- vitamin B_6 6–8 mg;
- pantothenic acid 20 mg;
- vitamin C 300 mg;
- vitamin E 20 mg.

Vitamins are very sensitive substances, and their effect can be lost if food is heated or wrongly prepared. A triathlete's diet should therefore include a high proportion of uncooked foods. Fresh whole foods are also very much preferable to industrially manufactured products.

Rules for preserving vitamins and minerals

- Wash foods whole so as to prevent too many vitamins and minerals from being flushed away.
- Wash all food in cold water. The shorter the washing time, the better the vitamins and minerals are retained.
- Where possible eat foods fresh and uncooked.

Symptoms of water loss according to the percentage of body weight lost

1–5%	6–10%	11–20%
thirst	dizziness	delirium
discomfort	headache	cramps
loss of mobility	breathlessness	swollen tongue
loss of appetite	pins and needles in the limbs	inability to swallow
flushed skin	lowered blood volume	hardness of hearing
impatience	raised blood concentration	blurred vision
fatigue	failure to salivate	wrinkled skin
raised pulse	bluish skin colour	pain in urinating
raised temperature	speech problems	numbness in the skin
nausea	inability to walk	failure to urinate

- Cook vegetables in only a small amount of water, and use the liquor as well.
- Don't keep food warm for too long, as this destroys the enzymes.
- Store all fruit and vegetables in a cool dark place.

Minerals and trace elements

Minerals and trace elements are inorganic substances that the body requires. If more than 100 mg of a certain element is needed per day, then it is known as a mineral. If less than 100 mg is needed, it is called a trace element.

Minerals usually occur in the form of electrically charged ions. They are important for preserving the electrical balance in the cell membranes and maintaining the osmotic pressure (the fluid concentration in and around the cells of the body).

The sweating associated with long endurance events leads to shortages of certain vital minerals, especially potassium and magnesium. Magnesium in particular must be replaced, and not only because it is vital to health. Regular magnesium intake alone has been shown to produce a marked improvement in performance. However, the daily dose should never be more than 10–20 mg, as excess magnesium can cause diarrhoea.

Trace elements have so far been little investigated. However, iron deficiency is known to affect the performances of female triathletes adversely. Zinc and selenium are thought to be important as anti-oxidants. Investigations have revealed a shortage of zinc in 80% of high-performance athletes, and this is thought to be the reason why such athletes are so liable to infection.

Vitamin sources and their importance to the human body

Water-soluble vitamins

Vitamin	Sources	Importance
vitamin B_1 (thiamin)	wheatgerm, rolled oats, yeast, wholemeal products, pork, pulses	carbohydrate metabolism; anti-oxidant
vitamin B_2 (riboflavin)	milk, meat, cereals, yeast, wheatgerm	energy production in the cells
vitamin B_6 (pyridoxine)	cereals, meat, liver, yeast, fish	protein metabolism, anti-oxidant
vitamin B_{12} (cobalamin)	all animal products	formation of red blood cells
vitamin C (ascorbic acid)	fresh fruit and vegetables (citrus fruit, rose hips, potatoes, sweet peppers)	connective tissue formation; anti-oxidant
folic acid	green leafy vegetables, wheatgerm, liver, yeast	amino-acid metabolism
pantothenic acid	a wide variety of plant and animal products	anti-oxidant
niacin	pork, yeast, wholemeal products, potatoes	energy production in the cells
biotin	soya flour, liver, yeast; also produced by intestinal bacteria	enzyme constituent

Fat-soluble vitamins

Vitamin	Sources	Importance
vitamin A (retinol)	liver, fish-liver oil, milk products, egg-yolk	vision; skin and mucous membranes; growth
provitamin A (ß-carotene)	carrots, sweet peppers, tomatoes, apricots, lettuce etc	vision; skin and mucous membranes; growth
vitamin D	liver, fish-liver oil, egg-yolk; formed in the skin under the influence of sunlight	calcium metabolism; bone formation
vitamin E	wheatgerm, wholemeal products, eggs, vegetable oils, brown rice, vegetables	fatty-acid metabolism (anti-oxidant)
vitamin K	many different foods, also produced by intestinal bacteria	blood clotting

General nutritional advice

A great number of the diseases that afflict our society today can be attributed to unhealthy diet. The chief causes are:

- too many foods that are full of "empty calories";
- too little dietary fibre such as can be found in wholemeal products, fresh fruit and vegetables;
- not enough vitamins, minerals and trace elements;
- too many chemicals that are dangerous to health.

Foods to avoid:

1. Sugar, or food and drink that is high in sugars:
   - monosaccharides (glucose, fruit sugar);
   - disaccharides (beet sugar, cane sugar, malt sugar, milk sugar);
   - sugary foods (sweets, chocolates, jams, biscuits etc);
   - sugary drinks (lemonade, coke etc).
2. Foods made from refined flour:
   - white bread, rolls, toast etc;
   - cakes, biscuits etc.
3. Other refined products such as white rice.
4. Foods containing a lot of fat:
   - all fried foods;
   - macaroni or egg noodles;
   - sausages and bacon;
   - egg yolk (fat and cholesterol).
5. Alcoholic drinks.

Recommended items:

1. Foods that are high in complex carbohydrates (polysaccharides or starches), together with the vitamins, minerals and trace elements that are needed to digest them.
2. Foods that are rich in high-quality proteins but low in fat.
3. Foods that contain fats with a high proportion of polyunsaturates.
4. Vegetables, fresh or dried fruit and fruit juices, all of which are rich sources of vitamins, minerals, trace elements, fluid and dietary fibre.

Pre-competition diet

The week leading up to a major competition is specially important as far as diet is concerned. The aim at this stage is to store up as much carbohydrate as possible in the system. Given the right diet, it is possible to increase glycogen stores from the usual 300 g up to 600–750 g, which is enough to keep you going throughout the whole length of the short triathlon.

There are several ways of boosting glycogen stores – or carbohydrate loading, as it is called. But all these methods have one thing in common: the diet in the last three days is high in carbohydrates but low in proteins and fats.

Method one

A week before the event, the athlete undergoes a heavy training session to deplete his glycogen stores – for example, a 15 km run at maximum intensity, or a 50 km cycling trial, or two long sessions of running or cycling at medium intensity. This is followed by a strict diet of fat and protein with a minimum of carbohydrate, which keeps the glycogen stores depleted. Then the high-carbohydrate diet is imposed for the last three days before the event.

This so-called Saltin Diet has proved highly effective in boosting glycogen stores. But for some people, two sudden diet changes within a week can spark off

Mineral elements and their importance to the human body

Element	Sources	Importance
sodium (Na)	cooking salt, smoked and salted foods	extracellular osmotic pressure; bioelectric system; enzyme function
potassium (K)	a variety of vegetable products	intracellular osmotic pressure; bioelectric system; enzyme function
chlorine (Cl)	cooking salt, smoked and salted foods	extracellular osmotic pressure; stomach acid
calcium (Ca)	milk, milk products, vegetables, fruit, cereals	bone structure; neuro-muscular excitation; muscle contraction; blood clotting
magnesium (Mg)	wheatgerm, pulses, poultry, fish, vegetables, fruit	bone structure; enzyme activation; muscle function
phosphorus (P)	milk, meat, cereals, fish, eggs	bone structure; cell structure; energy supply; membrane function

digestive problems and cause drastic fluctuations in weight. It is therefore not suitable for everyone, and should always be tested out first before being adopted for a major competition.

Method two
This method is generally similar to the previous one, but there are two important differences: firstly, the heavy training session to deplete glycogen stores takes place only four days before the event; then the fat-and-protein diet is dispensed with and carbohydrate loading begins immediately.

The main disadvantage of this method is that the heavy training session is so close to the event itself. Some athletes may not be quite fit enough to recover properly before the event takes place.

Method three
The third option is to manage without carbohydrate loading during the week preceding the event. There is less training in this week anyway, so that glycogen stores will be at least up to normal. The better trained an athlete is, the more fat he will burn up during the competition, and the less he will be dependent on large stores of glycogen.

Trace elements and their importance to the human body

Element	Sources	Importance
silicon (Si)	bran, plant fibre	bone structure; connective tissue and cartilage formation
zinc (Zn)	peas, cheese, eggs, meat, fish, liver, oranges	growth; sexual function; skin structure; healing processes; appetite
iron (Fe)	liver, brewer's yeast, wholemeal products, chives, parsley, broccoli, sprouts	enzyme constituent; oxygen transport
manganese (Mn)	cereals, spinach, berries, pulses	bone and cartilage formation
fluorine (F)	meat, eggs, fruit, vegetables	teeth and bone structure
copper (Cu)	liver, pulses, nuts	elastic fibres (main blood vessels); bone structure; blood formation
iodine (I)	eggs, milk, sea fish	thyroid function; physical and mental development
selenium (Se)	meat, fish, brewer's yeast, wholemeal products, fruit, vegetables	anti-oxidant; muscle function; blood clotting

Diet on the day

Here are some basic rules to follow:

- Don't change your diet habits on the day of the competition itself (ie never try anything you haven't tried during training).
- Never start an event with an empty stomach.
- Eat your last meal 2–3 hours before the start; choose food that is easily digestible; eat slowly and chew your food well.
- Choose foods that are high in carbohydrates (muesli, wholemeal products, bread, fruit).
- Avoid glucose immediately before the start, as the sudden rise in blood sugar will stimulate the production of insulin, leading eventually to a drop in blood sugar.
- Don't drink too much; in hot weather, drink an extra half-litre about half an hour before the start.

During the event

Eating during the event will provide extra energy, but this is only necessary for competitions that last more than 2–3 hours. Extra water is all that is needed for a short triathlon.

Competitors in the middle triathlon should eat while cycling, whereas those in the long triathlon should eat while running as well. Bananas and muesli or energy bars are the best carbohydrate sources. Many triathletes prefer sugary drinks like Coca Cola because these give them "instant energy". Regular liquid (water) intake is essential for all athletes while cycling and running.

Alexandra Kremer's diet during the 1986 German Championships
(2.5/99/25)
(air temperature 30°C in the shade)

- in the hour preceding the event: 1 bottle (½ litre) of magnesium-rich mineral water;
- while cycling: 2 litres of water (4 bottles), 1 banana and 1 energy bar;
- while running: 0.1 litres of water at every refreshment point (every 1.5–2 km);
- at the finish: plenty of mineral water containing magnesium, potassium and iron.

After the event

When the event is over, a high-carbohydrate meal is needed in order to replenish glycogen stores. Fluids, vitamins, minerals and proteins must also be replaced.

In the hours immediately following a competition, there is a dramatic change in the body's metabolism, in which *catabolic* (breaking-down) processes give way to *anabolic* (building-up) processes. During this period the body is particularly receptive to the nourishment that it requires.

The following menu is recommended in order to replenish the body's supplies in the right proportions:

1. First eat a portion of high-carbohydrate food that is nourishing but easily digestible, such as potatoes, brown rice or wholemeal products; in hot weather eat some fresh fruit salad or compôte as well.
2. Then eat a small portion (about 125 g) of low-fat, high-protein food, such as poultry, fish, lean beef or veal (vegetarians should replenish proteins

with low-fat quark, cottage cheese, egg-white and pulses).
3. The best desserts are fresh fruit (oranges, grapefruit, bananas etc) or fresh fruit salad, maybe mixed with quark or yogurt (a popular athletes' dessert).
4. Afterwards drink about half a litre of fruit juice, either neat or diluted with water half-and-half; don't drink anything more until later, or your stomach will be too full, preventing the digestive juices from working properly.

The basics of a healthy diet

- Follow a varied diet of mixed foods.
- Avoid sugar and refined products.
- Avoid salt, as this may cause high blood pressure.
- Eat plenty of dietary fibre in your food.
- Avoid too much fat and cholesterol, and keep to unsaturated fats.
- Diet to remove excess body weight, but not by fasting as this reduces performance and endurance capacity.
- Eat little and often throughout the day so as to keep variations in blood sugar level to a minimum.
- Cook without salt, and with a minimum of fat; eat vegetables raw wherever possible.
- Avoid alcohol, tobacco and caffeine.

Hot weather

Human performance is greatly influenced by both heat and humidity, especially in endurance sports.

The body's internal temperature is normally 37°C (98.4°F). Variations of only a few degrees can be damaging to health, so the body has various ways of keeping its temperature constant. The muscular activity associated with sport produces heat, and the only way to stop the body temperature rising is by dispersing this heat into the environment (air, water, ground etc), whether by conduction, convection, radiation or evaporation.

If the air temperature rises, then these dispersal processes will increase accordingly. There is more sweating, and blood flow to the skin is increased. As more blood is circulated to the skin, less is pumped around the kidneys, liver and working muscles, which means that lactic acid levels are raised and performance is reduced.

Most body heat is dispersed by the evaporation of sweat from the skin. Increased sweating in hot weather means that a large amount of fluid is lost. The symptoms of fluid loss are described on page 112. Triathletes competing in hot countries such as Hawaii can lose as much as 6–10 litres of sweat within the space of three hours. If these losses are not replaced, then the effects may be serious or even life-threatening. So it is vital for both athletes and coaches to be familiar with the dangers of competing in hot conditions.

Heat exhaustion

The athlete becomes confused and the skin becomes pale and clammy. The pulse rises to above 100 bpm, while the blood pressure is lowered and the blood temperature is raised. The person affected should be kept cool; he should rest in a horizontal position with the head slightly raised, and must drink plenty of fluids.

Heatstroke

Heatstroke is a much more drastic form of heat exhaustion involving a complete physical collapse. All the body's functions start to break down. The skin is dry and flushed, and the body temperature may rise to as high as 40°C (104°F) in some cases (body cells can only survive temperatures above 41°C (106°F) for a very short time).

The danger of heatstroke increases with age. The condition is even more likely when an athlete has used stimulants to push his performance beyond his own physical limits. Heatstroke is lethal and requires immediate medical treatment.

Sunstroke

Sunstroke is an irritation of the outer brain membranes (meninges) due to an excess of sunlight, especially on the head and neck. The symptoms are nausea, sickness, dizziness and stiffness in the neck. The problem can be treated by placing the victim in a cool, shady place and applying cold compresses.

Heat cramps

These are particularly common among inadequately trained athletes. Salt losses due to heat lead to stomach and muscle pains, vomiting, cramps and general debility. Regular endurance training reduces the amount of salt lost in sweat. Salts lost during exercise can be replaced afterwards by means of electrolyte drinks that are low in sodium and high in potassium.

Acclimatisation

Heat symptoms can best be prevented by an acclimatisation period of at least 4–5 days. The body adapts more quickly when training than when at rest. Acclimatisation training should preferably be in the morning or at the time when the competition is due to take place. The athlete should spend at least four hours a day in the sun (protected against sunburn), and should consume an adequate supply of fluids, minerals and vitamin C. The training pulse rate is high at first, but drops noticeably by the third or fourth day. Blood volume and sweating are increased, and fewer salts are lost during sweating. The athlete feels generally better overall.

Danger!

Hot weather can be dangerous if:

- the air temperature is above 25°C (77°F);
- the humidity is more than 70%.
- the wind speed is less than 0.4 m/s (1 mph or force 1).

Rules for competing in hot weather

- Allow a long enough period for acclimatisation.
- Drink large amounts of fluid before, during and after an event.
- During the event watch out for any signs of overheating that may have serious or even lethal consequences (throbbing headache, dizziness, extreme muscle weakness, hair standing on end).
- Compete at lower speeds to prevent excess lactic acid build-up, which occurs at lower speeds in hot conditions.
- Avoid alcohol, coffee, medicines or drugs.
- Don't compete if you are not fully fit, if you are under stress or recovering from an infection, even a mild one.
- Keep throwing water over your head, neck and legs to keep them cool (at every refreshment point).

Swimming in cold water

The human body also has a variety of mechanisms for reducing heat loss to keep the internal temperature up to around 37°C (98.4°F). Water absorbs and conducts heat much more effectively than air. One litre of water can absorb 3,200 times more heat than the same volume of air, while the thermal conductivity of water is 25 times that of air. So heat is lost much more quickly through water than through air.

The body reacts to cold by producing greater amounts of energy to make up the heat loss. But even in water at 20°C (68°F) the body is no longer able to prevent a fall in its internal temperature (that of the brain and vital organs). Only a limited period can be spent in the water before hypothermia sets in.

Swimming through cold water speeds up the heat loss even more. Physical activity increases the blood flow to the skin, encouraging further heat loss. The swimmer also enters new areas of cold water that have not yet been heated by his body. Heat loss varies from one swimmer to another, depending mainly on the thickness of the fat layer under the skin. Well-trained athletes usually have the worst problems because they have less fat.

The body can adapt to the cold by making the heat sensors in the skin react less to sensations of cold. This can be encouraged by taking a cold shower every day, having regular saunas, and swimming in unheated pools, and in open water later in the year. The metabolic rate can also be increased so as to produce more heat, but this requires regular and prolonged exposure to cold water over a considerable period.

The only certain way to reduce heat loss is by wearing a neoprene suit (see page 17). A lot of heat is lost through the head, so a neoprene cap is also advisable.

No swimming should be allowed if the water temperature is below 14°C (57°F). If it is below 17°C (62.6°F), then swimming should be limited to 1,000 m. The course should never be longer than 1,200 m until the water temperature reaches the so-called tolerance level of 20°C (68°F).

It is also worth noting that diving into cold water increases both the systolic and diastolic blood pressure. Measurements of as high as 300 over 150 are perfectly possible. Older or less well-trained athletes should take particular note of this fact.

Jet-lag

The human body is accustomed to a regular alternation between day and night, and between wakefulness and sleep. The body has a kind of internal biological clock that responds to external stimuli such as daylight. The associated body rhythms are called circadian rhythms, and these are known to affect performance. Research shows that the body performs best between eight and ten in the morning. Performance then falls off until three in the afternoon, then rises to another peak between five and six in the evening.

The time changes associated with long flights cause a phenomenon known as jet-lag, in which the biological clock no longer corresponds to the actual time. Performance suffers until the body's rhythms have adjusted to the new time.

Sleep and eating rhythms take up to a week to adjust, or about a day for every two hours' time difference. The central nervous system also adapts fairly quickly, so that technique does not suffer for very long. But the same is not true of the so-called vegetative nervous system that controls such processes as hormone production.

A long adjustment period is needed when you fly from Europe to North or South America, the Far East or Australasia. You should travel there at least a week, or preferably two or three weeks, beforehand, and resume training as soon as possible. One way of adapting more quickly is to anticipate the change beforehand. You can start to adapt your routine a few weeks before travelling, gradually adjusting your sleeping and training times so that they become closer to the times in the place you are going to.

Drugs and medicines

There have always been people who have used drugs to try to enhance their performance. There are many reasons why this should happen, among top athletes especially – overweening ambition, economic necessity, social or national prestige, or simply the desire to suppress pain during training and competition.

Doping can be defined as attempting to enhance an athlete's performance by non-physiological means – ie by the administration of a drug, whether by the athlete himself or by an assistant, either before or during a competition, or (in the case of anabolic steroids) during training.

The manipulation of sports performance through drugs is to be condemned for the following reasons:

■ Doping goes against the central principle of fairness upon which sportsmanship is based. Athletes are no longer competing on equal terms.

- The enhancement of performance by means of drugs means that sporting achievements can no longer be attributed to an athlete's own physical prowess.
- Sports teaching in education is only acceptable so long as parents can be sure that their children are being taught responsibly.
- Manipulation of performance through drugs is often damaging to health.

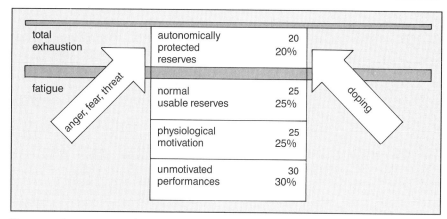

total exhaustion	autonomically protected reserves	20 20%
fatigue	normal usable reserves	25 25%
	physiological motivation	25 25%
	unmotivated performances	30 30%

anger, fear, threat

doping

Human performance capacity.

Performance potential is only 80% realisable by means of willpower alone. The remaining 20% of performance capacity lies outside the area of conscious control, and is protected by various autonomic processes. The so-called autonomic reserves can only be tapped in extreme circumstances, such as when a person is in great danger or in the grip of strong emotions such as anger or fear.

Drugs can provide access to these reserves that are not normally available. They break through the natural barrier of fatigue so that an athlete performs far beyond his normal limits, leading eventually to total exhaustion. The result is a complete physical collapse, often with lethal consequences.

The dangers of drug abuse are always greater in sports such as the triathlon that make very heavy demands on performance. The most common abuses in the triathlon are the use of psychomotor stimulants, the use of medicines to make an athlete "fit again" after illness, and the use of painkillers, especially during the final run. Pain is the body's natural way of protecting itself against overuse injuries. The use of painkillers suppresses this natural barrier,

and also alters the blood-flow characteristics.

The use of any drug to enhance performance is therefore to be deplored. This applies to *all* drugs used for this purpose, including many that have not so far been included on the list of banned drugs (see overleaf).

Heavy penalties are imposed on triathletes who give a positive reading in dope tests. They are banned for life from international competition, and for a minimum of three years from all domestic triathlon events. Because the triathlon is associated with the controlling boards of swimming, cycling and running, the ban extends to these sports as well.

The IOC Medical Commission's official list of banned doping classes and methods 1988

Doping Classes

A Stimulants
B Narcotics
C Anabolic Steroids
D Beta-blockers
E Diuretics

Doping Methods

A Blood doping
B Pharmacological, chemical and physical manipulation

Classes of Drugs subject to certain restrictions

A Alcohol
B Local anaesthetics
C Corticosteroids

NB The doping definition of the IOC Medical Commission is based on the banning of pharmacological classes of agents.
The definition has the advantage that also new drugs, some of which may be especially designed for doping purposes, are banned.

The following list represents examples of the different dope classes to illustrate the doping definition. Unless indicated all substances belonging to the banned classes may not be used for medical treatment, even if they are not listed as examples. If substances of the banned classes are detected in the laboratory the IOC Medical Commission will act. It should be noted that the presence of the drug in the urine constitutes an offence, irrespective of the route of administration.

Doping Classes

CLASS A: Stimulants

For example:

amfepramone
amfetaminil
amiphenazole
amphetamine
benzphetamine
caffeine*
cathine
chlorphentermine
clobenzorex
clorprenaline
cocaine
cropropamide (component of "micoren")
crothstamide (component of "micoren")
dimetamfetamine
ephedrine
etafedrine
ethamivan
etilamfetamine
fencamfamin
fenetylline
fenproporex
furfenorex
mefenorex
methamphetamine
methoxyphenamine
methylephedrine
methylphenidste
morazone
nikethamide
pemoline
pentetrazol
phendimetrazine
phenmetrazine
phentermine
phenylpropanolamine
pipradol
prolintane
propylhexedrine
pyrovalerone
strychnine

and related compounds

*For caffeine the definition of a positive depends upon the following: − if the concentration in urine exceeds 12 micrograms/ml

Stimulants comprise various types of drugs which increase alertness, reduce fatigue and may increase competitiveness and hostility. Their use can also produce loss of judgement, which may lead to accidents to others in some sports. Amphetamine and related compounds have the most notorious reputation in producing problems in sport. Some deaths of sportsmen have resulted even when normal doses have been used under conditions of maximum physical activity. There is no medical justification for the use of 'amphetamines' in sport.

One group of stimulants is the sympathomimetic amines of which ephedrine is an example. In high doses, this type of compound produces mental stimulation and increased blood flow. Adverse effects include elevated blood pressure and headache, increased and irregular heart beat, anxiety and tremor. In lower doses, they e.g. ephedrine, pseudoephedrine, phenylpropanolamine, norpseudoephedrine, are often present in cold and hay fever preparations which can be purchased in pharmacies and sometimes from other retail outlets without the need of a medical prescription.

THUS NO PRODUCT FOR USE IN COLDS, FLU OR HAY FEVER PURCHASED BY A COMPETITOR OR GIVEN TO HIM SHOULD BE USED WITHOUT FIRST CHECKING WITH A DOCTOR OR PHARMACIST THAT THE PRODUCT DOES NOT CONTAIN A DRUG OF THE BANNED STIMULANTS CLASS.

Beta2 agonists

The choice of medication in the treatment of asthma and respiratory ailments has posed many problems. Some years ago, ephedrine and related substances were administered quite frequently. However, these substances are prohibited because they are classed in the category of "sympathomimetic amines" and therefore considered as stimulants.

The use of only the following beta2 agonists is permitted in the aerosol form:

bitolterol
orciprenaline
rimiterol
selbutamol
terbutaline

CLASS B: Narcotic analgesics

For example:

alphaprodine
anileridine
buprenorphine
codeine
dextromoramide
dextropropoxyphen
diamorphine (heroin)
dihydrocodeine
dipipanone
ethoheptazine
ethylmorphine
levorphanol
methadone
morphine
nalbuphine
pentazocine
pethidine
phenazocine
trimeperidine

and related compounds

The drugs belonging to this class, which are represented by morphine and its chemical and pharmacological analogs, act fairly specifcally as analgesics for the management of moderate to severe pain. This description however by no means implies that their clinical effect is limited to the relief of trivial disabilities. Most of these drugs have major side effects, including dose-related respiratory depression, and carry a high risk of physical and psychological dependance. There exists evidence indicating that narcotic analgesics have been and are abused in sports, and therefore the IOC Medical Commission has issued and maintained a ban on their use during the Olympic Games. The ban is also justified by international restrictions affecting the movement of these compounds and is in line with the regulations and recommendations of the World Health Organisation regarding narcotics.

Furthermore, it is felt that the treatment of slight to moderate pain can be effective using drugs – other than the narcotics – which have analgesic, anti-inflamatory and antipyretic actions. Such alternatives, which have been successfully used for the treatment of sports injuries, include Anthranilic acid derivatives (such as Mefenamic acid, Floctafenine, Glafenine, etc.) Phenylalkanoic acid derivatives (such as Diclofenac, Ibuprofen, Ketoprofen, Naproxen, etc.) and compounds such as Indomethacin and Sulindac. The Medical Commission also reminds athletes and team doctors that Aspirin and its newer derivatives (such as Diflunisal) are not banned but cautions against some pharmaceutical preparations where Aspirin is often associated to a banned drug such as Codeine. The same precautions hold for cough and cold preparations which often contain drugs of the banned classes.

NOTE: DEXTROMETHORPHAN IS NOT BANNED AND MAY BE USED AS AN ANTI-TUSSIVE. DIPHENOXYLATE IS ALSO PERMITTED.

CLASS C: Anabolic steroids

For example:

bolasterone	methyltestosterone
boldenone	nandrolone
clostebol	norethandrolone
dehydrochlormethyl-	oxandrolone
testosterone	oxymesterone
fluoxymesterone	oxymetholone
mesterolone	stanozolol
metandienone	testosterone**
metenolone	

and related compounds

***Testosterone:* the definition of a positive depends upon the following – the administration of testosterone or the use of any other manipulation having the result of increasing the ratio in urine of testosterone: epitestosterone to more than 6:1.

It is well known that the administration to males of the Human Chorionic Gonadotrophin (HCG) and other compounds with related activity leads to an increased rate of production of androgenic steroids. The use of these substances is therefore banned.

This class of drugs includes chemicals which are related in structure and activity to the male hormone testosterone, which is also included in this banned class. They have been misused in sport, not only to attempt to increase muscle bulk, strength and power, when used with increased food intake, but also in lower doses and normal food intake to attempt to improve competitiveness.

Their use in teenagers who have not fully developed can result in stunting growth by affecting growth at the ends of the long bones. Their use can produce psychological changes, liver damage and adversely affect the cardio-vascular system. In males, their use can reduce testicular size and sperm production; in females, their use can produce masculinisation, acne, development of male pattern hair growth and suppression of ovarian function and menstruation.

CLASS D: Beta-blockers

For example:

acebutolol	nadolol
alprenolol	oxprenolol
atenclol	propranolol
labetalol	sotalol
metoprolol	

and related compounds

The IOC Medical Commission has reviewed the therapeutic indications for the use of beta-blocking drugs and noted that there is now a wide range of effective alternative preparations available in order to control hypertension, cardiac arrythmias, angina pectoris and migraine. Due to the continued misuse of beta-blockers in some sports where physical activity is of no or little importance, the IOC Medical Commission reserves the right to test those sports which it deems appropriate. These are unlikely to include endurance events which necessitate prolonged periods of high cardiac output and large stores of metabolic substrates in which beta-blockers would severely decrease performance capacity.

CLASS E: Diuretics

For example

acetazolamide	diclofenamide
amiloride	ethacrynic acid
bendroflumethiazide	furosemide
benzthiazide	hydrochlorothiazide
bumetanide	mersalyl
canrenone	spironolactone
chlormerodrin	triamterene
chlortalidone	

and related compounds

Diuretics have important therapeutic indications for the elimination of fluids from the tissues in certain pathological conditions. However, strict medical control is required.

Diuretics are sometimes misused by competitors for two main reasons, namely: to reduce weight quickly in sports where weight categories are involved and to reduce the concentration of drugs in urine by producing a more rapid excretion of urine to attempt to minimise detection of drug misuse. Rapid reduction of weight in sport cannot be justified medically. Health risks are involved in such misuse because of serious side-effects which might occur.

Furthermore, deliberate attempts to reduce weight artificially, in order to compete in lower weight classes or to dilute urine, constitute clear manipulations which are unacceptable on ethical grounds. Therefore, the IOC Medical Commission has decided to include diuretics on its list of banned classes of drugs.

NB For sports involving weight classes, the IOC Medical Commission reserves the right to obtain urine samples from the competitor at the time of the weigh-in.

Doping Methods

A: Blood doping

Blood transfusion is the intravenous administration of red blood cells or related blood products that contain red blood cells. Such products can be obtained from blood drawn from the same (autologous) or from a different (non-autologous) individual. The most common indications for red blood transfusion in conventional medical practice are acute blood loss and severe anaemia.

Blood doping is the administration of blood or related red blood products to an athlete other than for legitimate medical treatment. This procedure may be preceded by withdrawal of blood from the athlete who continues to train in this blood depleted state.

These procedures contravene the ethics of medicine and of sport. There are also risks involved in the transfusion of blood and related blood products. These include the development of allergic reactions (rash, fever etc.) and acute haemolytic reaction with kidney damage if incorrectly typed blood is used, as well as delayed transfusion reaction resulting in the fever and jaundice, transmission of infectious diseases (viral hepatitis and AIDS), overload of the circulation and metabolic shock.

Therefore the practice of blood doping in sport is banned by the IOC Medical Commission.

B: Pharmacological, chemical and physical manipulation

The IOC Medical Commission bans the use of substances and of methods which alter the integrity and validity of urine samples used in doping controls. Examples of banned methods are catheterisation, urine substitution and/or tampering with urine, inhibition of renal excretion, e.g. by probenecid and related compounds.

Classes of Drugs Subject to Certain Restrictions

CLASS A: Alcohol

Alcohol is not prohibited. However breath or blood alcohol levels may be determined at the request of an International Federation.

CLASS B: Local anaesthetics

Injectable local anaesthetics are permitted under the following conditions:

a) that procaine, xylocaine, carbocaine, etc. are used but not cocaine;
b) only local or intra-articular injections may be administered;

c) only when medically justified (i.e. the details including diagnosis; dose and route of administration must be submitted immediately in writing to the IOC Medical Commission).

CLASS C: Corticosteroids

The naturally occurring and synthetic corticosteroids are mainly used as anti-inflammatory drugs which also relieve pain. They influence circulating concentrations of natural corticosteroids in the body. They produce euphoria and side-effects such that their medical use, except when used topically, require medical control.

Since 1975, the IOC Medical Commission has attempted to restrict their use during the Olympic Games by requiring a declaration by the team doctors, because it was known that corticosteroids were being used non-therapeutically by the oral, intramuscular and even the intravenous route in some sports. However, the problem was not solved by these restrictions and therefore stronger measures designed not to interfere with the appropriate medical use of these compounds became necessary.

The use of cortiocsteroids is banned except for topical use (aural, opthalmological and dermatological), inhalational therapy (asthma, allergic rhinitis) and local or intra-articular injections.

ANY TEAM DOCTOR WISHING TO ADMINISTER CORTICOSTEROIDS INTRA-ARTICULARLY OR LOCALLY TO A COMPETITOR MUST GIVE WRITTEN NOTIFICATION TO THE IOC MEDICAL COMMISSION.

Digestive problems

Digestive problems are a common cause of unpleasantness during training and competition. The following points should be noted if such problems are to be avoided:

- The digestion has to work hardest about an hour and a half after the consumption of a high-carbohydrate meal (the period is longer after a high-protein or high-fat meal). So the last big meal should be taken at least 2–3 hours before exercise begins.
- Carbohydrates make fewer demands on the digestive tract than fats or proteins.
- High-protein and high-fibre foods (vegetables and salads) should be avoided before competitions.
- A completely empty stomach can be just as bad as a full one. Hunger feelings such as cramp, nausea and emptiness can have an adverse effect on performance. So it is sometimes sensible to have a small meal of easily digestible carbohydrates about a half to one hour before a competition or training session.

Wanting to empty your bowels, especially while running, can be due to a number of causes. Sometimes the mere movement or shaking of the body is enough to set it off. In some athletes this is due to the enlargement of the groin muscles, which then tend to "massage" the colon. Other causes may be drinking coffee or overconcentrated electrolyte drinks or fruit juices, or the excitement before the competition, or simply the effect of cold.

Careful observation is the best way to pinpoint the causes of digestive problems during physical exercise – taking careful note of what is eaten and the body's reaction to it.

The stomach can often react badly to cold food or drinks after vigorous exercise. The first meal after a competition should be easily digestible, and should not be taken until the symptoms of exhaustion have largely subsided.

Some athletes may benefit from taking a purgative twice a year (though not during the competition period). A recommended dosage is 50 g of sodium sulphate (Glauber's salt) or magnesium sulphate (Epsom salts) in 1.5–2 litres of lukewarm water. The diet in the days following should consist mostly of vegetables and cereal products.

One of the commonest problems is an unpleasant "stitch" or pain in the side. This is usually caused by eating too much before vigorous exercise. The full stomach contracts painfully as it is buffeted around by the movement of the body. A stitch can also be due to faulty breathing or stretching of the interlacing capsules in the liver and spleen. Only very rarely does a stitch mean that exercise should be stopped.

Injuries

There are two categories of sports injury that may occur in the triathlon: overuse injuries and injuries due to accidents.

Overuse injuries

Performance capacity in the triathlon is limited among other things by the physical load capacity of the body's supportive and connective tissues. If the physical demands of training and competition are not matched to an athlete's individual capacity, then the body becomes overloaded. Incorrect training methods may also have the same effect. The result is a series of chronic minor injuries, leading eventually to more general physical damage.

If there are pains in any moving parts of the body that cannot be attributed to obvious injury, then these must be treated as symptoms of overuse. They usually go away quickly when the pressure is taken off. But they should always be taken as a sign of possible underlying problems that may not yet be apparent. Such problems may include:

Postural problems to do with the spine
These often lead to muscle shortening or muscle weakness, resulting in cramps and pains during training. The best way of dealing with such problems is a programme of special exercises designed to strengthen the back muscles.

Legs of unequal length
This problem is indicated when the pelvis is crooked and the spine is bent sideways to compensate. It can be treated by means of specially measured (orthopaedic) shoes, which prevent further injuries from occurring.

Bow legs and knock knees
These can lead to overuse injuries in the knees, ankles and feet. Bow legs put extra pressure on the inside of each knee joint; knock knees affect the outside. Both can result in chronic problems such as loose ligaments, cartilage problems and wearing of the joints. Minor cases can be dealt with by means of simple shoe adjustments (see page 35). But in more extreme cases an operation is needed to straighten the legs.

Foot problems
Foot problems are by far the commonest cause of chronic overuse injuries. If the arches are fallen lengthways, the feet usually turn outwards with the heel bones turned inwards. This can result in injuries to the ligaments, tendons and muscles, and to the ankle, knee and hip joints. Such overuse injuries can be prevented if the foot muscles are strengthened by means of shoe inserts, special foot exercises and running barefoot on soft ground.

Splayfoot is the result of arches that are fallen crossways. It puts a lot of stress on the middle of the metatarsal bones, where corns and callouses may develop. Apart from foot exercises, special shoe inserts are needed. These provide soft padding under the main big toe joint, some assistance for the first metatarsal bone, and support for the arch.

Foot problems are often associated with various toe deformities. The commonest of these is the bunion, in which the big toe is pushed outwards at the base. Serious bunions must be treated by means of an operation.

Foot-strengthening exercises

1. Sit and bend your feet as far as they will go; then straighten them up again. Use weights as you become more proficient. (10 repetitions with the right and left foot alternately.)
2. Sit with your feet flat on the ground. Raise the inside and outside edges of your feet alternately as far as they will go, and hold them there for 10 seconds apiece (10 repetitions).
3. Stand on tiptoe, and slowly roll your feet onto your heels and back onto your toes again. Hold for a few seconds at either end of the movement (10 repetitions).
4. Try to pick up objects with your toes.
5. Alternately bend and stretch your toes, holding for a few seconds at either end of the movement. (10 repetitions with the left and right foot alternately.)

Tendon problems

The function of tendons is to transfer power from the muscles to the joints via the bones. Tendons are liable to a number of different painful conditions, which come under the general heading of tendopathy. Overuse injuries of the tendons are almost as common as muscle injuries. Damage can occur at the base of a tendon (insertion tendopathy), in the tendon tissues (peritendinosis) or in the sheath around the tendon (tendovaginitis).

Apart from overuse during training, tendon problems can be due to a variety of causes: acute injuries from kicks or blows when tensed; inclement weather (they don't stretch so easily when it is cold and damp); psychological factors (tiredness or lack of concentration); faulty technique or unsuitable equipment; or a pre-existing condition such as damage from cortisone treatment.

The result may be tendonitis. The tendon becomes swollen and inflamed, losing its elasticity and shock-absorbent qualities. Reduced blood supply causes a build-up of lactic acid and irritates the sensitive nerve endings. The resulting pain is aggravated by exercise. The affected muscles become blocked, and in extreme cases there is calcification around the base of the tendon.

Achilles tendon problems

The most frequent site for tendonitis in triathletes is the Achilles tendon, which is particularly vulnerable during running. The cause may be no more than pinching from an ill-fitting heel tab, or faulty technique due to malfunctioning ligaments or a foot deformity.

The inflamed tendon should be treated with ice packs, soothing dressings, ultrasound and electrotherapy. A heel insert in the shoe will reduce the strain on the tendon. Training should be reduced, and running should be stopped altogether for a while. In extreme cases an operation is needed in order to remove damaged tissue. The condition can, however, be prevented by regular stretching exercises, relaxing calf massages and wearing shoes with a flat heel wedge.

Achilles tendon pain can also be caused by a condition known as heel spur, in which the knob at the back of the heel bone becomes thickened. This happens when the make-up of the heel causes the Achilles tendon to pull too hard on the heel bone. The inflammation should be treated, and the pressure on the heel should be reduced by wearing shoes that are open or have a soft heel counter. In severe cases the heel spur can be reduced by surgical means.

Other tendon problems

Another unpleasant condition is tendovaginitis of the foot extensor muscles. This may be caused by a blow to the instep or by rubbing from a tight shoelace. The problem can be dealt with by careful padding of the instep after the inflammation has died down.

If there is pain along the inside of the shin bone (shin splints), this is most often due to insertion tendopathy of the lower leg muscles. This problem is associated with excessive pronation (flat feet that turn outwards). The muscles affected are the tibialis posterior and the long flexors of the toes. (See also stress fractures below.)

Treatment again is mainly a question of removing the cause of the condition, whether by replacing the shoe, by using a heel insert and a shoe insert to provide medial support, or by correcting the running style. The inflammation can be treated with ice packs, soothing dressings, anti-inflammatory drugs and muscle relaxation exercises.

Bursitis

A bursa is rather like a small cushion of water. Bursae are found in places where muscles and tendons run across a bone, and act as a pad to protect them from damage. However, they too can become inflamed.

The commonest such condition is bursitis around the kneecap, generally known as housemaid's knee. This can be caused by long cycle rides in the cold and wet, especially early in the year. Visual symptoms include redness, hotness and swelling, while the joint becomes painful to touch or to move.

Running can cause bursitis in the hip joint (over the large ball at the top end of the thigh bone). This should be treated with ice packs, anti-inflammatory lotions and a rest from training. If the condition becomes chronic, it may be advisable to remove the bursa surgically. This does not cause any problems, as a new bursa forms around the joint.

Stress fractures
Tiny stress fractures are becoming increasingly common, especially among young runners. This is thought to be caused by training programmes that involve excessive training loads or inappropriate postures. The bones most often affected are the second metatarsal in the foot, the tibia (shin bone) and fibula (calf bone), and the talus (keel bone) at the base of the foot.

Shin splints may be due to tendon problems (see above) or periostitis (inflammation of the outer bone membrane), but they may also be a sign of a stress fracture. If so, the training load must be reduced for at least 2–3 months to allow the bone to heal properly. The best solution in the triathlon may be to concentrate on swimming and cycling for that period.

Preventive measures
The following procedures will reduce the risk of overuse injuries occurring:

- Compensation measures to correct inappropriate posture, preferably under the guidance of a skilled orthopaedist with an interest in sport. (Some manufacturers of orthopaedic shoes are already using a treadmill and a video camera to analyse foot movements; this can be a very useful exercise.)
- Improving technique and avoiding unnatural movements.
- Starting every training session with intensive warm-up exercises, including loosening-up and stretching exercises.
- Careful planning of individual training

sessions: heavy exercises should be placed at the beginning of the main session, and a proper warm-down is never a waste of time.
- A suitable diet, and plenty of rest after training, enhanced by recovery aids such as sauna or massage.
- Special foot and back exercises to prevent overuse injuries in those areas.
- Detailed information about every item of equipment, especially the running shoes (see page 34).
- Good medical back-up, including appropriate physiotherapy.

The triathlon is less liable to overuse injuries than many other sports. This is partly because of the variety of training involved (over-specialised training often predisposes to injury). Many runners switch to the triathlon because of a long history of chronic injury problems. If these problems recur, swimming and cycling provide a means of continuing training without any loss of general fitness.

Acute injuries

Swimming injuries
Swimming injuries are relatively few in comparison with those in other sports. Swimmers in open water can sometimes injure themselves on various nasty objects such as wood, iron nails or glass. Triathletes most often complain of chills, and of grazes and blisters caused by rubbing from neoprene suits. The latter can be prevented by rubbing vaseline over affected areas. If the middle ear becomes inflamed (otitis media), then no swimming should be allowed.

Cycling injuries
Cycling is the most dangerous part of the triathlon, because it often involves riding

in traffic. Being careful is the only way to prevent accidents. Fortunately the most common injuries are fairly superficial. Cuts and grazes account for 62% of injuries, followed by bruises and strains with 26%. The majority of serious injuries involve bone fractures or head injuries. In 19% of accidents the head is injured in some way.

Cycling injuries in the triathlon
- cuts and grazes 62%
- bruises and strains 26%
- serious head injuries 4%
- fractures (especially to the arm and collar bone) 8%

A large proportion of severe head injuries can be avoided by wearing a good crash hat made of hard plastic. Crash rings mostly provide protection from cuts and grazes. Safety pedals can also be an advantage in a crash, because they are so easy to get out of quickly in emergencies (see page 23).

Running injuries
The most frequent running injuries are ankle sprains and bruises. When an ankle is sprained outwards, this often damages the capsules and ligaments around the outside of the joint.

Running injuries in the triathlon
- sprains and bruises 58%
- fractures 11%
- cuts 8%
- other injuries 23%

Causes of injury in the triathlon
Two major causes of injury in the triathlon are fatigue and loss of concentration due to the long duration of the event. Technical shortcomings no doubt add to the number of injuries. Triathletes cannot

be expected to reach the same level of expertise as specialists in the three constituent disciplines. But the problem is aggravated at present by a lack of well-trained coaches who can provide expert guidance.

The risk of injury is greatly minimised by careful training and preparation before a difficult event, and by the right behaviour during the event itself. Common sense and individual responsibility are particularly important in the triathlon.

Types of injury in the triathlon

- skin damage   32.6%
- muscle damage   25.0%
- sprained joints   23.0%
- bruises   8.0%
- fractures   8.0%
- ruptured ligaments   6.0%
- bursa injuries   6.0%
- cartilage damage   2.0%

Muscle damage

Muscle injuries are among the commonest injuries to occur in the triathlon. If there is no more than *myalgia* ("sore muscles") – slight damage to the protein cords that make up the muscle fibres – then this is not treated as an injury.

However, *muscle stiffness,* in which the muscle tone is increased in some parts of the muscle, is already on the way to becoming an injury. If the affected muscle is not treated with relaxing massage, contrast baths and stretching exercises, then further exercise may lead to a *pulled muscle,* in which some of the fibres get torn. They soon heal, leaving a scar, but without any loss of function.

A severe strain can lead to a *muscle tear,* in which a much greater number of fibres are torn. This should be treated

immediately with ice packs, a compression bandage and support to relieve pressure on the muscle. The muscle should not be exercised again until it is completely free of pain.

In very severe cases a *muscle rupture* occurs, in which a large part of the muscle is torn apart. The condition is obvious from a depression under the skin. Surgery may be necessary in order to knit the muscle back together. If the muscle is left to heal by itself, the scar tissue may be so extensive that muscle function becomes limited or completely absent.

Muscle cramps are not an injury as such. They usually occur when a particular muscle group has been overworked so that it is starved of fluid, minerals or oxygen. The problem can be eased by carefully stretching and relaxing the affected muscle, or maybe rubbing it with an ice pack, until the pain eases.

Skin damage

Skin injuries are an everyday occurrence for most athletes. Superficial *cuts and grazes* occur most often during cycling. Clean or superficial wounds need only to be treated with a suitable disinfectant. If a wound is deeper or gets dirty, it will need medical treatment. An anti-tetanus injection is also advisable.

Small abrasions in the seat area can easily become irritated by creases in the leather insert of cycling shorts, or by sweating or rubbing from a plastic seat. This may result in boils or even abscesses. These can be relieved with soothing antiseptic creams and daily herbal baths. However, such problems can be avoided altogether by using the right saddle, by wearing a good leather insert that is kept regularly greased (eg with vaseline), and by careful bodily hygiene.

Blisters occur mostly during running. They can be lanced using a sterile needle. When the fluid has drained away, the skin should be disinfected. The old skin should be left on so as to protect the new skin that is forming underneath. Further blistering can be prevented by rubbing the affected areas with vaseline.

If a runner suffers *bleeding under a toenail,* this must be treated by a doctor, who will make a hole at one or more points to drain the blood from underneath. The affected toe is then dressed and bandaged (the nail need not be removed).

Bruises and sprains

If the torso area is bruised by a heavy blow from a blunt object, then there is a danger of internal injuries underneath (spleen, liver, kidneys or arteries). So if a cyclist has crashed, then a very thorough examination is necessary.

The initial treatment is the same for bruises, sprains (usually of the ankle) and tendon injuries in the feet and hands. The affected part should be supported in a raised position, and cooled with ice packs or with running water for at least half an hour. It should then be wrapped in a compression bandage and given plenty of rest. An X-ray should be taken to make sure there are no fractures or torn ligaments.

For the next 4–6 weeks, a supportive bandage that also allows movement will help protect against further injury. If there are any torn ligaments in the ankle or knee, then surgery will be required.

Ruptured tendon

This can occur if sudden tension is applied by a muscle to an already damaged tendon. When this happens to the Achilles tendon, it is accompanied by a loud snap. Immediate surgery is necessary before the muscle becomes shortened. Ice packs should be applied until surgery is possible.

Torn cartilage

The knee contains a number of C-shaped structures each made of cartilage and known as meniscuses. These act as shock absorbers and help to distribute pressure during exercise. If the knee is badly twisted, then a piece of cartilage may be torn or ripped away. If the meniscus hasn't been damaged before, then arthroscopy is the usual procedure: a thin tube is inserted through the joint capsule, and the offending piece of cartilage is removed with a fine instrument. Otherwise an operation is necessary in order to remove the damaged meniscus.

Colds and other infections

Top athletes, especially in endurance sports, are much more liable to infection than the population at large. They are particularly susceptible to infections of the upper respiratory tract, such as colds and sore throats. These annoying complaints effectively shorten the training period, and cause a marked deterioration in competition performances.

A number of reasons can be given for the increased susceptibility to infection in competitive sports:

- Certain minerals may be lacking in the diet, such as magnesium, zinc or iron.
- Increased respiration may expose the athlete to more germs.
- The mucous membranes may provide less protection, whether because of

increased blood supply or because they have dried out.
- The athlete often becomes chilled.
- Stress may raise the levels of a hormone called hydrocortisone (cortisol), with possible adverse effects on the body's immune system.
- The immune system may be weakened by certain metabolic changes, such as the breakdown of protein or the build-up of lactic acid.

Researches carried out by Ricken and Kindermann revealed the following information about competitive athletes:

- a lack of lysozyme, responsible for non-specific bodily immunity;
- a reduction in T-lymphocytes, responsible for specific cellular immunity;
- reduced levels of immunoglobulin, responsible for the body's general immunity;
- a lack of zinc and magnesium in 70% of cases.

Susceptibility to infection is such a common reason for athletes dropping out of training and competitions that the treatment of infections is becoming increasingly important as an element of training.

However, a number of measures can be taken to prevent such infections in the first place:

- Eat a healthy and nutritious diet.
- Take food supplements to correct deficiencies, such as a daily dose of magnesium.
- Rub a suitable ointment in your nostrils to prevent the mucous membranes from drying out.
- Avoid extreme changes in temperature or situations that are liable to cause chills.
- Have plenty of sleep.

There is a whole range of medications available which may help in the prevention and treatment of infections. Apart from the usual conventional remedies, there are a number of "natural" or homeopathic preparations, though most of these have yet to be scientifically tested for effectiveness.

If any infection leads to temperature, then exercise should be stopped altogether until the fever has died down. This warning applies especially to endurance sports, including the triathlon. This is because many of the infective agents involved can also cause inflammation of the heart muscle (myocarditis).

Vigorous exercise under such circumstances, whether in training or competition, can cause permanent damage to the heart. Symptoms such as disturbed heart rhythms may accompany the person for the rest of his life. He may even have to give up sport altogether, or at the very least he will never achieve his previous performance level.

So even flu, if neglected, can develop into a life-threatening illness. Fortunately myocarditis can be readily diagnosed by means of an ECG (electrocardiogram) test.

Women's problems

In most traditional sports it was a very long time before women were admitted into official championships. They were not allowed into the Olympics until 1928, and in the 1968 Olympics in Mexico City the longest women's running distance was still only 800 m. The triathlon is in total contrast to this in that women have taken part from the very beginning, and have always competed over the same distances as men.

There are a number of basic differences between the sexes, resulting from various anatomical, physiological and psychological factors. Women as a whole possess the following characteristics in relation to men:

- lower stature (13 cm/5 in less on average);
- lower body weight (by 20–25%);
- higher overall percentage of body fat;
- lower proportion of muscle tissue;
- lighter bone structure;
- muscles that can be stretched more easily;
- less strength in the ligaments and connective tissues;
- good coordination;
- lower levels of energy production;
- smaller heart and lung capacity;
- lower blood pressure;
- smaller number of red blood corpuscles and lower haemoglobin level.

Female characteristics in relation to body weight appear to give them certain advantages, especially in the area of endurance capacity. However, there are variations in both training and performance capacity that are closely related to the menstrual cycle.

Since the late seventies an increasing number of investigations have been carried out into the effects of physical exercise on female hormone function. This was because of certain evidence which suggested that prolonged periods of endurance training might be the cause of certain changes in the menstrual cycle, such as:

- delayed menstruation (eg every 40–45 days);
- anovulatory cycles (menstruation without ovulation);
- amenorrhoea (absence of menstrual periods).

A whole range of possible causes has been adduced, most of which tend to reinforce one another:

- excessive intensity and/or volume of training;
- low body weight, low proportion of body fat (<8%), large weight loss;
- previous menstrual irregularities;
- pregnancy as yet undetected;
- heavy physical and/or emotional stress, social factors;
- nutritional deficiencies.

The menstrual irregularities that affect women triathletes can simply be treated as normal. They have not so far been found to have any adverse effects on health. If the training programme is reduced, regular menstruation usually returns without any further ill effects.

If osteopororis (bone wasting) occurs, or there are recurrent infections of the urinary tract, then hormone treatment may be considered.

The effect of hormone changes on performance capacity varies enormously from one woman to another, and it is impossible to make any generalisations.

Loss of blood during menstruation means that women need much more iron than men. And because iron is neither absorbed nor stored in any quantity, it is important to prevent iron deficiency. A simple iron-vitamin supplement is advisable during periods of heavy exercise (50–60 g per tablet). This should be taken for 3–4 weeks, then stopped for a rather longer period. The haemoglobin level should be measured regularly; and if this falls below 125 g/l, the iron level should also be checked.

Medical examination

Anyone wishing to train for the triathlon would be advised to have a full medical and orthopaedic examination. The purpose of this is to check for any underlying illness, or for any skeletal abnormality that may predispose towards overuse injuries.

Vigorous exercise should not be undertaken if any of the following defects are present:

- congenital or inherited heart defects;
- severely disturbed heart rhythms;
- high blood pressure if untreated;
- acute or chronic infectious illnesses;
- metabolic problems if untreated or not effectively cured (hyperthyroidism, diabetes);
- organic changes that may make exercise risky (liver, lungs, kidneys);
- previous instances of bleeding from the gullet, stomach or intestine.

Untreated dental problems can also affect performance adversely (tooth decay, gum disease, wisdom tooth problems or other types of inflammation). The increased carbohydrate intake (mineral drinks, muesli bars etc) makes endurance athletes particularly liable to such problems. It is therefore important to clean teeth and gums carefully, to have regular dental check-ups, and to have any problems treated immediately.

Some sports-medicine institutes carry out a complete medical examination of athletes in their care, especially those in the top rank. Not only is their health thoroughly examined, but their performance capacity is measured;

Mother and child? – perfectly feasible even in top-level sport.

a prognosis is also made of their anticipated future performance, and their training programmes are planned accordingly.

A number of requirements must be fulfilled for an athlete to be able do well in a heavy endurance sport such as the triathlon. He must be in perfect health; he must have the right physical profile, good technical ability and the correct biomechanical characteristics for the sport concerned; he must also have both the motivation and the opportunity to undertake an extensive programme of training that concentrates primarily on developing aerobic endurance. This in turn relies on a good oxygen supply and the most efficient utilisation of that supply.

Aerobic performance capacity can be measured from the maximum oxygen intake ($\dot{V}O_2$ max) in relation to body weight, or indirectly from the number of watts produced for every kilo of body weight. The efficiency of oxygen utilisation in the working muscle can be worked out from the blood lactate measurement. This is because lactate values are an indirect indicator of the degree of oxygen debt in energy metabolism.

A large amount of data must be obtained in order to make a prognosis of anticipated future performance. One decisive factor is the heart size in relation to the volume of blood that it is capable of handling. Measurement of the aerobic-anaerobic threshold allows one to make an indirect prognosis of oxygen utilisation in the muscle, because this is limited by the proportion of slow-twitch muscle fibres (ie those that favour aerobic energy supply).

Field tests must be carried out in each sporting discipline separately in order to plan the training programme effectively. These tests are repeated several times during the course of the training year, and the volume, intensity and methods of training are adjusted accordingly. Some measurements can be most effectively made by the athlete himself (general state of health, weight, pulse rate), while urine and blood tests should be carried out by the sports doctor in charge. Pulse rates are measured in relation to the exercise undertaken.

Sports medical parameters for top German male athletes in 1986

	average	minimum	maximum
age (years)	26	19	39
body weight (kg)	75	63.6	90.2
body height (cm)	181.9	168	194
proportion of body fat (%)	12.64	8.2	14.9
heart volume (ml)	1,228.7	981	1,597
heart rate at rest (bpm)	55.6	42	71
heart rate under maximum pressure (bpm)	186.2	168	197
vital capacity (litres)	5.85	4.72	6.73
respiration value (%)	83.4	74	95.7
respiration volume (litres/min)	176.1	145.5	204
maximum performance (watts)	403.3	366.6	433.3
maximum performance (W/kg)	5.43	4.62	5.95

Appendix

Organising a triathlon event

As the triathlon becomes ever more popular, more and more competitions are being added to the triathlete's calendar. But if you are thinking of organising such an event, it is important to be aware of the amount of planning and effort that is needed to bring it off.

Preliminary planning

Initial planning should start as much as a year in advance of the event. A preliminary plan of action should be carefully worked out, including not only the course and the event itself, but detailed budget and sponsorship proposals. Every event depends ultimately on finances. Entry fees from competitors are often simply not enough on their own to provide adequate finance, so help will be needed from sponsors.

Securing sponsorship is a task in itself, and some initial publicity will be needed in order to woo sponsors in the first place. Many firms will be interested in sponsoring the event because they see it as an opportunity for advertising their products. The triathlon may provide a new outlet for marketing their wares, especially if these include equipment, clothing or refreshments that are directly related to the event.

Some firms may also be in a position to undertake some aspect of the planning, such as a catering firm providing refreshments. But apart from such things as refreshments and T-shirts, none of this will be directly related to the comfort of the competitors themselves. So further effort and publicity will be needed to make the event attractive to potential competitors.

Planning the triathlon course is another of the important tasks to be done initially. The different possibilities depend very much on local geography. First a stretch of water is needed, such as a lake, a river, a canal or an area of sea. After that there is the business of deciding what lengths of course to include. Should it be a people's triathlon (0.5/20/5 km), a short triathlon (1.5/40/10 km) or a middle triathlon (2/80/20 km)? The choice will again depend partly on local geography.

Before you can start planning in earnest, you must first get permission from various authorities to stage the event (the cycling course is a particularly sore point here). There are a large number of formalities to be gone through, such as insurance cover, an undertaking to observe the traffic regulations, and submitting a detailed description of the course, including maps. And this is the minimum that will be required to satisfy the local authorities.

Other bodies must also be notified, such as the police authorities and the local emergency and rescue services. Cross-country routes may require the permission of landowners and other responsible bodies, whether local or national. The Forestry Commission must be notified, for example, if the route passes through areas under their control.

Provided none of these groups raises any objections, the planning and preparation can go ahead. Some permits, however, are not issued until close to the event itself, so one must carry on planning without these.

It is usually worth seeking the cooperation of more long-standing sports organisations in the district, whose experience will be invaluable in getting the event off the ground. One person alone cannot hope to control everything, so tasks will need to be delegated and responsibility shared between interested parties. The ideal situation is a joint effort organised by three existing clubs, who can each bring the benefit of their long experience of organising long-distance swimming, cycle touring and marathon events. Each club can then be responsible for its own part of the course, and can be represented on the central coordinating committee.

The rest of the planning can begin just as soon as all the backup arrangements have been set in motion, such as permits, sponsorship, committee structure etc. Now is the time to begin the detailed planning of the actual event (swimming, cycling, running, changing facilities etc). Different areas of work must be allocated to various individuals or subcommittees – general planning, media relations, continuity and coordination of the various activities, provision of equipment, and construction and dismantling of stands, marquees etc.

After the first few meetings, a detailed plan of action can be drawn up, together with a list of equipment required. As planning progresses, some tasks will be accomplished and may be crossed off the list, while others will carry on right up to and beyond the event itself. The latter will include such tasks as media communications and cooperation with the various authorities.

The number of helpers needed on the day will vary between 100 and 300, depending on the size of the actual event. Triathlon organisers have found from experience that helpers work best if they are fully informed about everything that is going on. Indeed, the main points should preferably be provided in a written document that can be easily referred to. Not only are the helpers better motivated if they know how they fit into the planning as a whole, but they are better placed to deal with queries from competitors.

Swimming and starting orders

For organisational reasons, it is advisable to limit the number of participants to 200 or 300 at the very most. This is to ensure that everyone can compete on equal terms. If more people take part, then the timing should be staggered, with separate groups starting at regular planned intervals.

It is best to start in the water, at the point where the swimmers are just out of their depth. A final explanation and run-down of the route should be given immediately before the start. The local lifeguards should be ready and on hand to deal with emergencies.

Relevant rules

- All swimmers must wear caps, and the starting number should be marked on the cap and on the upper arm of each swimmer.
- Neoprene suits and protective goggles may be worn.
- Any outside help, private companions or short cuts are forbidden.
- There is no restriction on swimming styles.
- Swimming aids such as paddles or flippers are forbidden.

Equipment needed

- numbered bathing caps (if possible in loud colours);
- starting line, starting pistol;
- security boats;
- marker buoys along the route;
- special marker buoys or boats placed at turning points;
- swimming lanes along the final stretch;
- showers for after sea swims.

The first intermediate time is given as each swimmer leaves the water. In order to time competitors accurately, swimming lanes should be marked out along the final part of the course, each of which should be just wide enough for one swimmer.

Changing zone

The changing area is a vital part of the planning. A smooth change-over will make the participants happier and spare a lot of annoyance and complaints.

It is simplest to organise just one changing area. But this is only possible if the cycling and running course both start and finish at the same place. Ideally there should be a large changing tent or marquee. Numbered benches can then be set out inside the marquee, so that each participant has his own place where he can change and leave his kit.

Not only will a tent provide protection against the weather and marauding photographers, but it can also be used for other purposes if the weather is bad (reception, refreshments, prize-giving etc). If a marquee is impossible for financial reasons, then the changing area should at least be screened off.

The changing area should be strictly out-of-bounds to all spectators and well-wishers. The only people to be allowed access are the competitors and their official helpers (who should have specific identification). The helpers will be needed in particular to help athletes change out of their neoprene suits.

The area must be carefully laid out to waste the minimum of participants' time. There should be plenty of space to avoid congestion, a separate entrance and exit, and clear signposting to help athletes find their way about. The changing zone between the swimming and cycling courses should have a refreshment stand immediately next to it, providing water, lukewarm tea and pieces of banana, plus another stand offering first aid and massage treatment.

If such ideal arrangements are impossible, then each participant should be issued with three large, sturdy plastic bags, each marked with his starting number and a large **S** (for swimming), **C** (for cycling) or **R** (for running). The swimming and cycling bags can then be placed in the first changing area, while the running bags are transported by the organisers to the running start. Though cheaper, this solution requires considerably more effort and planning, and there is a much greater danger of mix-ups occurring.

Equipment needed

- changing tent with numbered benches;
- or failing that screens and plastic bags;
- bananas, water, tea.

Cycling

Cycle stands will be needed for the bicycles. These can be made out of strips of wood. Iron or wooden bars can be used just as effectively, or even a tightly stretched length of cord which the brake levers can be hooked over.

The cycles are ranged according to each rider's starting number. They can be numbered using adhesive labels or painted numbers on the cycle stands. The numbers can either be enclosed with the participants' starting documents, or else allocated by the organisers immediately before the race.

Modern bicycles are expensive machines, and must be carefully cordoned off; only the cyclists and their helpers should be allowed near them. At the end of the course a numbered ticket should be issued as the bicycle is surrendered. This procedure will take twice the effort to organise if the start and finish are in different places.

Planning a cycling course is no easy task. The route should be set out neatly with brightly coloured arrows (red or orange) to help the riders to find their way. The whole course should be carefully checked out a few hours before the event.

Safety is paramount, and is not always easy to ensure. All crossroads and right turns should be carefully guarded, preferably with the assistance of the police. All danger spots should be marked with large warning signs such as

Food and refreshment must be carefully organised so that no time at all is wasted.

DANGER – CROSSROADS, DANGER – RIGHT TURN, DANGEROUS EXIT or DANGER – SHARP BEND. Emergency services must be on hand in case of accidents, preferably with an ambulance parked near every danger spot.

Refreshment and control points will also be needed, although the number of them will depend on the length of the course (preferably at 20 km intervals). In the short triathlon, refreshment points can be dispensed with along the cycling section. In order to be readily visible, refreshment stands should be placed either at or just beyond the top of a slope, or else along a level stretch of road. Bananas should be provided, together with full ½–1-litre drinking bottles that

can be exchanged for the riders' empties.

Course supervision is another vital part of the organisation. Riders must be prevented from wheel-following. This is forbidden by the rules, as it gives an unfair advantage to the rider behind, who is protected from the wind by the rider in front. But there are always competitors whose ambition is greater than their sportsmanship, so the route must be continually supervised. Course judges on motor cycles are best placed to keep an eye on the riders. They can issue warnings through a megaphone, and if necessary disqualify any rider who is in clear breach of the rules (his number and the nature of his offence can be immediately spoken into a dictaphone).

Relevant rules

- A crash hat is compulsory.
- Cyclists must observe all the rules of the road.
- Wheel-following leads to automatic disqualification.
- All outside help is strictly forbidden.
- Cyclists may carry repair tools and spare tyres with them.

Equipment needed

- cycle stands;
- barricade equipment;
- cycle numbers;
- riders' starting numbers;
- bicycle tickets;
- arrows for the route;
- warning signs for danger spots;
- motor cycles for course judges.

The cycling section leads directly into the second changing period. The final section of the course should again be divided into lanes which allow only one rider through at a time. There must be assistants on hand to guide each bicycle into a lane. If there are enough assistants, the machine can then be placed in the appropriate numbered stand. Otherwise it can simply be placed according to the lane through which it arrived.

Running

By the time the final section of the race has begun, the athletes will already be very tired, and will not always be very alert. So it is important to mark out the route very clearly. Large white arrows should be chalked along the ground. Extra barricades may also be useful, and assistants to point out the way.

The route should preferably be traffic-free and firm to run on so as to minimise the risk of accidents. Good woodland paths are the most pleasant type of route, as they also provide shade in hot weather. The course should be well provided with refreshment points, offering water (in half-full beakers), wet sponges (to cool the skin) and pieces of banana.

Kilometre or mile posts are very much appreciated by the runners at this late stage in the race. First aid and ambulances should also be on hand. Exhaustion is by no means rare at this stage, especially in hot weather, and sometimes help is needed very urgently.

Relevant rules

- The starting number must be worn so that it is clearly visible from in front.
- Outside help, private assistance or running mates are strictly forbidden.

Equipment needed

- chalk or wood chippings to mark out the route;
- barricade tape and signposts;
- kilometre posts;
- refreshment stands with drinks, bananas, beakers, sponges and water containers.

The final time is given at the end of the run. Some laning is again essential in order to catch every participant on arrival. This saves all the unfairness and trouble caused when athletes have been accidentally missed.

Processing the results

Assessing the final results is an exacting task that requires good planning and a well-trained team of judges and scorers. The first essential is for the course judges to be able to time each competitor accurately and record his starting number correctly. If there are a large number of competitors, this will be impossible without a laning system.

People should work in pairs to enter the results from the control points along the route, with one person reading them out and the second person entering them on a carefully prepared list of competitors. The resulting lists of times are then processed via a computer that has been programmed for the task, or else typed out carefully in the order of final arrival times.

Immediately the first sheet of results is produced, another helper starts making photocopies (one for each competitor plus any other copies required). Meanwhile another group of workers (all with good handwriting) will be filling out the certificates. Some organisers save time at this point by handing out certificates for the competitors to fill in themselves (they should be handed out in transparent folders immediately on arrival at the finish). When the copies of the results list are ready, these can be enclosed with the certificates, together with a suitable covering document.

The office must at this stage be closed to everyone except those directly involved in these various processes. Otherwise the operation will be hampered by people interfering.

Other helpers in the meantime will be making final preparations for the prize-giving ceremony. A platform should already have been set up in a commanding position, with a speaker's stand and a table for displaying the prizes and medals in a decorative fashion. Prize-giving can begin as soon as the first results list is available. Public personalities are normally delighted to hand out the prizes.

Leaving the cycle park for the second part of the race.

A triathlon management plan

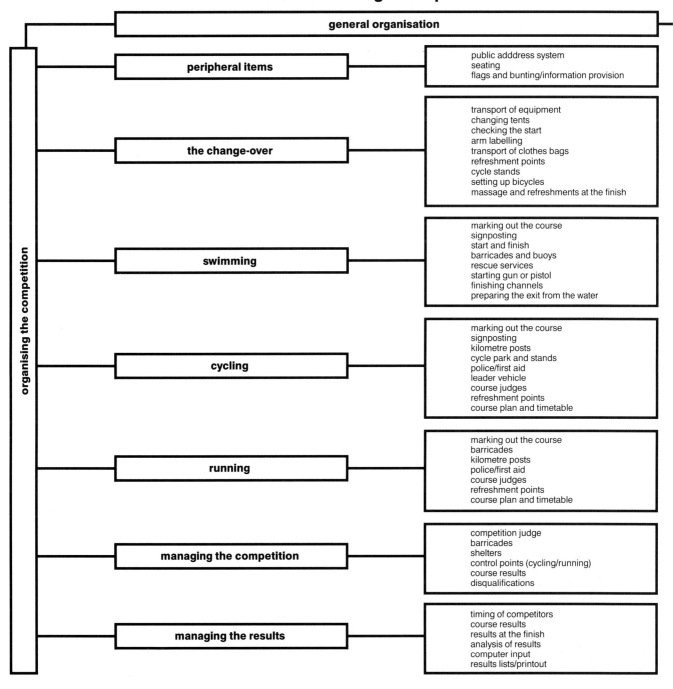

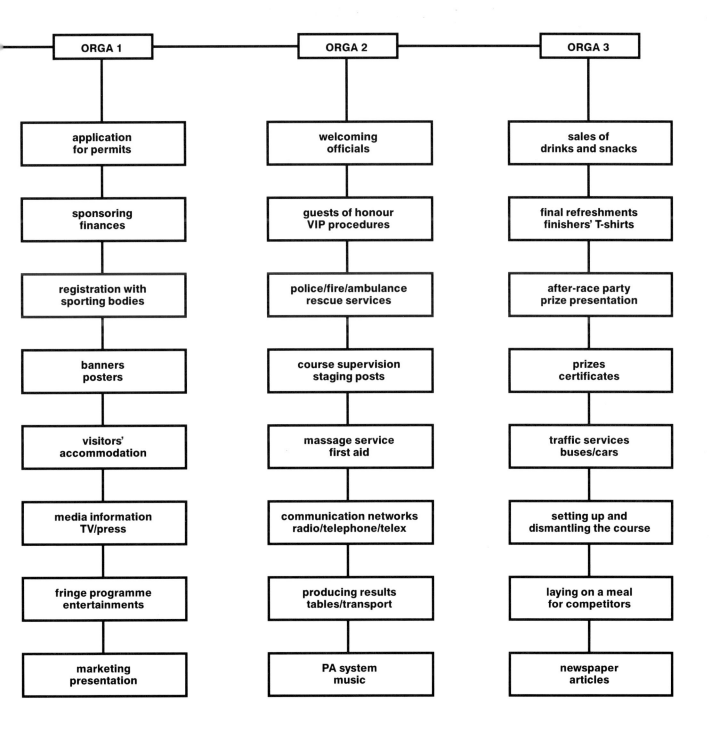

ORGA 1	ORGA 2	ORGA 3
application for permits	**welcoming officials**	**sales of drinks and snacks**
sponsoring finances	**guests of honour VIP procedures**	**final refreshments finishers' T-shirts**
registration with sporting bodies	**police/fire/ambulance rescue services**	**after-race party prize presentation**
banners posters	**course supervision staging posts**	**prizes certificates**
visitors' accommodation	**massage service first aid**	**traffic services buses/cars**
media information TV/press	**communication networks radio/telephone/telex**	**setting up and dismantling the course**
fringe programme entertainments	**producing results tables/transport**	**laying on a meal for competitors**
marketing presentation	**PA system music**	**newspaper articles**

Triathlon rules

BTA Competition rules
Published with the permission of the British Triathlon Association

The following rules shall apply to all events sanctioned by the Association. Any promoter seeking variances of these rules must apply in writing for dispensation, and all event literature shall clearly state any such variance.

1.   Promoters

All persons staging an event shall comply with all aspects of the current *Organising and Staging a Triathlon* booklet issued by the Association.

1.1 Promoters of all events run under the rules of the Association must apply for a Letter of Sanction from the Association.

1.2 All sanctioned events must be covered by insurance acceptable to the Association.

1.3 Only sanctioned events may qualify for cover under the Association's Event Insurance Policy.

1.4 Competitors in sanctioned events unable to produce a current Race Licence (issued by the Association) at registration for those events shall not receive a rebate on their entry fee, and will be deemed to hold a one-day licence. A one-day licence entitles the holder to third-party and personal accident insurance only while participating in the event.

1.5 A complete list of all persons entered in an event shall be available at time of registration.

1.6 A provisional results sheet containing names and times of competitors shall be displayed at the presentation ceremony.

1.7 A ratified results list shall be despatched to all persons who registered in an event, with a copy being forwarded to the Association, no later than thirty days after the competition. The ratified results list shall give details of time, position and any category status. Wherever possible split times shall be given.

2.   Swimming

2.1 The start signal shall be both audible and visual.

2.2 Competitors shall use no aids to swimming other than cap, goggles and costume. A costume may consist of a ''wetsuit'', providing that the hands and feet are not covered and the total thickness of the material (or materials) worn is no more than 3 mm.

2.3 Competitors may stand during the race, but shall not make progress along the course during this time other than is deemed necessary to execute entry into and exit from the designated swimming course. In shallow waters an exact point when swimming must commence and may cease shall be appointed and marked.

2.4 Competitors shall at all times swim so that they do not deliberately obstruct or interfere with other competitors. Making contact other than by accident shall be declared unsporting impedence.

2.5 All swimming sections shall have a time limit. The time limit will be specified on the briefing sheet and also given at the final briefing meeting. No safety cover shall leave the course or be withdrawn until instructed to do so by the safety officer.

2.6 At the end of the time limit any competitor still in the water shall be ordered to retire − at the discretion of the event referee.

2.7 All competitors shall wear a brightly coloured swim cap.

2.8 Competitors shall have their competition numbers clearly marked on their swimming cap and on the back of at least one hand.

2.9 No competitor will be allowed to continue until their competition number has been recorded at the exit point.

2.10 No competitor shall be permitted to continue who in the opinion of a race official is unfit to do so.

3.   Safety provision − swimming section

3.1 Straight-line courses over 1.5 km. On such courses every competitor shall be accompanied individually by a safety craft.

3.2 Straight-line courses under 1.5 km. Safety craft or platforms shall be stationed at 100 m intervals along the course, spaced from the back marker to 200 m in front of the lead swimmer. Additional boats/canoes shall patrol the swimming area to ensure that no swimmer is at any time more than 50 m from safety cover.

3.3 Circuit courses. Safety craft shall be spaced at 100 m intervals with canoe, boat or lifeguard backup so as to achieve a ratio of one safety unit per 20 swimmers. At no time should any swimmer be more than 50 m from a safety unit, even when craft are already engaged on recovery work.

3.4 A suitable craft shall act as a guide by maintaining station some 25 m ahead of the leading male and female competitor.

3.5 All turns shall be clearly marked by buoys or other forms of marking, these being clearly visible to the competitors.

3.6 The course shall be clearly marked every 50 m with a buoy or other marking device. Marker buoys shall be of a different colour from race hats.

4. Medical cover

4.1 At all championships a qualified medical practitioner is to be present.

4.2 First aid units in attendance are to be briefed by the medical officer on the requirements of treatment for shock and cold.

4.3 Sufficient blankets are to be on hand to supply a minimum of 20% of the entrants.

4.4 Re-heat facilities are to be on hand, together with a good supply of hot drinks.

5. Guidelines as to minimum water temperatures

5.1 Organisers in conjunction with their Race Director and Medical Officer should give careful consideration to using an alternative venue or reducing the distances when the water/air temperature falls below that which is considered safe.

5.2 The water temperature should be taken from a point in the middle of the course at a depth of 50 cm within one hour of the start, and should be announced to competitors at least 15 minutes prior to the start of the competition.

5.3 The recommended minimum temperature at which wetsuits should be optional is 14°C (57°F).

5.4 At temperatures of less than 14°C the wearing of wetsuits should be recommended and the following maximum distances should be considered:

- at 13°C (55°F): 2 km
- at 12°C (54°F): 1 km
- at 11°C (52°F): 500 m.

5.5 At temperatures of less than 11°C (52°F) it is recommended that no open-water swimming takes place.

5.6 The above guidelines are based on water temperatures alone and assume that the wind-chill factor is negligible.

5.7 Wherever practical, the ratio of the sections should be maintained when the swimming distance is shortened.

6. Cycling

6.1 Every competitor must make sure that their machine is in a safe and roadworthy condition. In particular, the machine must be fitted with two independent braking systems in good working order, with brake levers securely fastened to the handlebars in such a position as to enable the rider to apply the brakes while maintaining a normal riding position. If the machine is equipped with a fixed wheel with a locking device properly fitted, then the rear brake may be dispensed with. Tyres shall be in good condition, and tubular tyres must be securely fitted to the wheels by a suitable means of adhesion.

6.2 The use of recumbent machines, protective shields, windbreaks, bodywork or other substantial means of reducing wind resistance on machines is prohibited.

6.3 ''Low-profile'' machines are

permitted, but disc wheels may only be used on the rear of the machine.

6.4 Prior to the start of the event, each competitor will either: (a) provide the organiser with a signed certificate of roadworthiness for the machine (in which case spot checks may be carried out); or (b) submit the machine for inspection by a machine examiner. Details of which procedure is to be followed must be included with the race information.

7. Safety helmets

7.1 Cycling safety helmets approved by BSI, ANSI, Snell or equivalent standards must be fastened by competitors before mounting their bicycles and worn at all times during the cycling section of the event and not removed until they have dismounted.

8. Assistance

8.1 During the event, competitors are individually responsible for the repair of their machines. Any assistance received other than that provided by the organisers will result in disqualification.

8.2 No individual support by vehicle, bicycle or on foot is permitted except as provided by the organisers.

9. Numbers

9.1 Competitors must wear the race numbers provided by the organisers throughout the cycling section of the event, in such a way that they are clearly visible from behind and/or from the side (left or right as indicated in the race brief).

10. Completing the course

10.1 Any part of the course may be covered on foot, but on these occasions the competitors must carry or push their own machines.

11. Rules of the road

11.1 All competitors must follow the normal "rules of the road", obey all traffic signals and must follow any directions given by the police, race marshals or officials. Any infringement of the law and subsequent legal action is the sole responsibility of the competitor.

12. Pacing/drafting

12.1 Competitors shall on no account take pace from another cyclist or from a vehicle. The riders must ride alone, singly and not two abreast except for the purposes of overtaking, and must ride no closer than 5 m from a rider in front.

12.2 While overtaking another competitor, a rider must pass as widely and as quickly as possible. On no account must there be "racing" side-by-side on the course, and as soon as the front wheels are side-by-side the overtaken rider must drop back a minimum of 5 m behind.

12.3 The onus of dropping back is on the rider being overtaken.

12.4 The 5 m rule is a minimum distance, which may be increased at the discretion of the organiser. Details of any increase shall be provided in the race brief.

13. Running

13.1 No form of locomotion other than running or walking is permitted.

13.2 No individual support vehicles, cyclists or escort runners are allowed.

13.3 All competitors must wear a shirt, vest or tri-suit, shorts etc, and must have their issued race number securely fixed and clearly visible from the front at all times.

13.4 Competitors must follow the directions and instructions of all race officials.

14. Other general rules

14.1 Competitors are reminded that this is an individual endurance event, and that any teamwork which provides an advantage over other competitors is expressly forbidden.

14.2 Medical personnel have the absolute authority to remove a competitor from the race who in their opinion is physically incapable of continuing without sustaining physical damage or loss of life.

14.3 Any competitor bringing the sport into disrepute is liable to immediate disqualification from the event and possible loss of membership.

14.4 It is the responsibility of all competitors to navigate the prescribed course.

14.5 It is the responsibility of all competitors to report to the race director as soon as practicable any violations of these rules.

14.6 Teams. For a team to qualify for the team award under BTA National Championship rules, all its members must be paid-up members of the same BTA-affiliated club.

14.7 In the running and cycling disciplines, all competitors must wear clothing conforming to recognised tri-suit patterns or alternatively as acceptable to other authoritative bodies for those competitive events when participated in as dedicated activities.

15. Drug abuse

15.1 Substances proscribed by the IOC are banned by the BTA. Any participant in triathlon in Great Britain may be tested for proscribed substances at any time. Testing will be carried out by the Sports Council following standard procedures laid down by the IOC. Refusal to give a specimen or participate in a test will be considered equivalent to a positive finding. The penalties for unequivocal abuse of proscribed substances will be a total lifetime ban from the sport of triathlon in Great Britain.

15.2 Any individual, regardless of nationality, known unequivocally to have had a positive drug test for proscribed substances by the IOC will be banned from triathlon in Great Britain.

The British Triathlon Association can be contacted at the following address:

Ken Wood
BTA Secretary
9 Lea Springs
Fleet
Hants GU13 8AR

Index

A

accessories 29
Achilles tendon 124
acute injuries 125–127
age in relation to mobility 88
alternating training methods 76
arthroscopy 127
autogenic training 101
autonomic reserves 119

B

basic training 58
biological value (food) 110, 111
bleeding under nails 126
blisters 126
body temperature 117, 118
bottom bracket 22
bow legs 35, 123
brakes 28
breathing (swimming) 40, 44
bruises 126
build-up training 58
bunions 123
bursitis 124
buoyancy 39

C

carbohydrate loading 114, 115
carbohydrates 109–110, 114
cartilage injuries 127
centre-pull brakes 28
chain 24
chainline 24, 25
chainwheels 22
changers 23, 24
changing clothes 62
change-over zone 103, 132
checklist for competitions 102
circadian rhythms 118
circuit training 80–81
climbing technique (cycling) 49, 50
clothing 17, 33, 35
CO$_2$ cartridges 29
cold water 118
combined training 61, 62
competition day 102–105
competition methods of training 77
competition period 62, 64, 65

competition planning 131–134
competitions 99–107
competitive training 58
conditioning 55–97
continuous training methods 76
controlling training 90, 129
cornering 49–50
covered wheel 26
cranks 22
crash hat 34, 125
crawl stroke 40–45
cuts and grazes 126
cycle maintenance 31–32
cycling injuries 125
cycling shoes 33
cycling technique 45–50

D

derailleur gears 23
density of training 56
desensitising techniques 101
diet 106, 109–116
digestion problems 122–123
disc-type wheel 25
doping 118, 119
drinking bottle 29
drugs 118, 119
duration of training 56

E

endurance competitions 16
endurance training 75–78
equipment 17–35
extensor muscles 86

F

fartlek training 76
fatigue 88, 94
fats 109–110
flat feet 35, 123
flexibility 87–90
flexor muscles 86
fluid intake 111–112
forks 22
frame (bicycle) 19–21
freewheel sprockets 23
frequency of training 56–57
front changer 23
front forks 22

G

gear tables 49
gearing 47–49

glucose 109
glycogen 109

H

handlebar position 46
handlebars 21–22
headset 22
heat exhaustion 117
heatstroke 117
heel problems 124
history of the triathlon 12–14
home trainer 33
honking 50
hormone problems 128
hot weather 116
hubs 25
hypothermia 118

I

infectious illnesses 127
injuries 123–127
insertion tendopathy 124
intensity of training 56
interval training 77
introduction 9–16
iron 115, 128

J

jet-lag 118

K

knock knees 35, 123

L

legs, unequal 123
ligament tears 127
linoleic acid 110
long-term endurance 75
loosening-up exercises 88

M

macrocycle 66
magnesium 114
maximum strength training 78
medical examination 129–130
meniscus injuries 127
mental attitude 88
mental training 101, 107
microcycle 66
minerals 106, 109, 113–114
mobility training 87–90
motivation 100–101
muscle fibres 76, 78

muscle injuries 126
muscular endurance 79–85
muscular power 78

N

neoprene suit 17
nutrition 106, 109–116

O

odometer 29
overcompensation 55
overload, progressive 57–58
overtraining 94–97
overuse injuries 123–125

P

parasympathetic overtraining 96
peaking 99–101
pedalling technique 46–49
pedals 22, 23
people's triathlon 15
periodisation 61–62
peritendinosis 124
physiotherapy 107
planning an event 131–137
planning training 58–67
potassium 109, 114
preparation period 61–62, 64, 65
progressive overload 57–58
propulsion (swimming) 39
prognosis of performance 129, 130
progressive muscle relaxation 101, 107
pronation 35
proteins 109, 110–111
psychotonic training 101
pullbuoy 18
pulley rope 86

Q

quick-release 25, 26

R

racing bike 18–32
raised arches 35
rear derailleur 24
record-keeping 90–93
recovery 57, 106–107
relaxation techniques 101, 107
results 134
rims 25

roller training 32
rolling resistance 26
round pedalling 46–47
rules and regulations 138–140
running equipment 34–35
running injuries 125, 126
running shoes 34–35
running technique 51–53

S

saddle 28
saddle position 29, 30
safety precautions 131, 132, 133
safety pedals 23, 125
shoes 33, 34–35
short-term endurance 75
side-pull brakes 28
skin damage 126
spare tyres 29
spinal cord 123
splayfoot 123
spokes 25
sports injuries 123–127
sprains 126
sprockets 23, 24
staggered start 132
stand pump 28
start 103, 132
starting documents 103, 132
steering 21–22
stitch 123
strength training 78–87
stress fractures 125
stretching exercises 89–90
sunstroke 117
supination 35
suppleness 87–90
sweating 106, 112, 117
swimming equipment 17–18
swimming injuries 125
swimming start 103, 132
swimming technique 39–45
sympathetic overtraining 94, 96

T

tapering 99–101
technique 37–53
temperature 88, 117, 118
tendon injuries 124, 126
tooth problems 129
trace elements 109, 113–115
training 55–97
training diary 90–93

training examples 68–74
training structure 58–67
transition period 62, 64, 65
transmission (bicycle) 22–25
triathlon suit 17
tubular tyres 26, 27, 32
tyre changing 32, 61
tyres 26–28, 32

V

vitamins 109, 112–113
volume of training 56

W

warm-up 88, 103
water 106, 109, 111–112
water resistance 39
wheels 25–28
wind resistance 45
women's problems 127–128

Y

yoga 101
youth events 15